Konstantinos Kyriakopoulos

Network Performance Measurements

Konstantinos Kyriakopoulos

Network Performance Measurements

A Wavelet Analysis for Compression and Feature Extraction

VDM Verlag Dr. Müller

Imprint

Bibliographic information by the German National Library: The German National Library lists this publication at the German National Bibliography; detailed bibliographic information is available on the Internet at http://dnb.d-nb.de.

Cover image: www.purestockx.com

Publisher:
VDM Verlag Dr. Müller Aktiengesellschaft & Co. KG , Dudweiler Landstr. 125 a, 66123 Saarbrücken, Germany,
Phone +49 681 9100-698, Fax +49 681 9100-988,
Email: info@vdm-verlag.de

Zugl.: Loughborough, Loughborough University, 2008

Produced in USA and UK by:
Lightning Source Inc., La Vergne, Tennessee, USA
Lightning Source UK Ltd., Milton Keynes, UK
BookSurge LLC, 5341 Dorchester Road, Suite 16, North Charleston, SC 29418, USA

ISBN: 978-3-639-07089-7

Abbreviations and Acronyms

AARNET Australia's Academic and Research Network

AC Arithmetic Coding

ACF Autocorrelation Function

AFB Analysis Filter Bank

AMP Active Measurement Program

ASN.1 Abstract Syntax Notation One

ATM Asynchronous Transfer Mode

BM Birge – Massart proposed threshold

CAIDA Cooperative Association for Internet Data Analysis

CDF Cumulative Distribution Function

CoMo Continuous Monitoring

CRC Cyclic Redundancy Check

C.R. Compression Ratio

DCT Discreet Cosine Transfer

DNS Domain Name System

DWT Discrete Wavelet Transform

EZW Embedded Zero Tree Wavelet

FGN Fractional Gaussian Noise

FIR Finite Impulse Response

FTP File Transfer Protocol

FWT Fast Wavelet Transform

GK Gupta – Kaur proposed threshold

GPS Global positioning system

HSN Loughborough University's High Speed Network

ICMP Internet Control Message Protocol

IESG Internet Engineering Steering Group

IETF Internet Engineering Task Force

IP Internet Protocol

IPv6 Internet Protocol version 6

IPPM Internet Protocol Performance Monitoring

KS	Kolmogorov-Smirnov
LRD	Long Range Dependence
MASTS	Measurements at All Scales in Time and Space
MIB	Management Information Base
MPLS	Multi Protocol Label Switching
MRTG	Multi Router Traffic Grapher
MSE	Mean Square Error
MSS	Maximum Segment Size
MTU	Maximum Transmission Unit
NIMI	National Internet Measurement Infrastructure
NLANR	National Laboratory for Applied Network Research
NMI	Network Measurement Infrastructure
NMS	Network Management System
PNG	Portable Network Graphics
PSNR	Peak Signal to Noise Ratio
QMF	Quadrature Mirror Filters
RLE	Run Length Encoding
RR	Record Route
R/S	Rescaled Range Statistic
RTT	Round Trip Time
SFB	Synthesis Filter Bank
SMTP	Simple Mail Transfer Protocol
SNMP	Simple Network Management Protocol
STFA	Short Time Fourier Analysis
TCP	Transmission Control Protocol
TTL	Time-to-live
TTM	Test Traffic Measurements
UDP	User Datagram Protocol
VBR	Variable Bit Rate
WWW	Word Wide Web

Contents

List of Figures

List of Tables

CHAPTER 1

Network Management, Performance Monitoring and Measurement

1.1 Introduction

As years pass, computer networks become increasingly essential to the infrastructure of human society. Computer networks are being extensively used
from small-scale organisations, schools and businesses to corporations, gov-
ernment institutions, military organisations and can extend to the size of
intercontinental research and academic facilities [Ben05]. Due to the fact
that most organisations have a high degree of dependence on computer networks, failures or misconfigurations in the network will cause great loss in
their productivity, and as a consequence reduce their income.

The nature of a computer network is a complex construction comprised
of both hardware and software. A computer network can be described as an

1

organisation where many interactions occur between the hardware devices, such as routers, bridges, hubs and links, and the protocols controlling and co-ordinating these devices [KR03].

When a large number of network devices are interconnected to make up a computer network, it is highly probable that some of the network components may malfunction, may need to be optimised for the current network configuration or simply need to be repaired. Moreover, some network resources may be utilised more than the prescribed limit, causing bottlenecks in the network [KR03].

The task of a network administrator is to monitor the network in order to prevent or recover it from mishaps and maintain a healthy status for the network and each of its devices. As computer networks have grown in both size and complexity, so the task of managing and maintaining the healthy status of the network has become more important. Consequently, the network manager needs to have special tools for the purpose of monitoring, controlling and managing the network [San01].

In the following paragraphs, the concepts of network management and network performance monitoring are introduced and discussed. A variety of network performance metrics are being presented and examined later on.

1.2   Network Management

A definition of network management is given in [SM96]: "Network management includes the deployment, integration, and co-ordination of the hardware, software and human elements to monitor, test, poll, configure, analyse, evaluate, and control the network and element resources to meet the real-time, operational performance, and Quality of Service requirements at a reasonable cost."

Network management includes many areas and covers all layers of the communications protocol stack. Computer networks should be carefully designed, planned, installed and tested. After the initial set up and installation they should be frequently maintained and upgraded as necessary [San01].

Network management is used in various areas ranging from simple detection of a hosts status, to security monitoring and performance measurement. Some of those areas are quickly presented below [KR03].

- Detecting a flawed interface card of a host or router

- Monitoring the status of a host

- Managing link traffic in order to improve resource deployment

- Detecting rapid changes in the routing tables of routers

- Detecting possible network intrusions

- Monitoring the network performance

Network managers need software that will help them remotely monitor and control the managed elements. They also need a way of collecting diverse information and statistics from all the network devices spread all over the managed network. This type of software should give to the administrator the capability to change behavioural parameters of the network devices. For example, the administrator could add a new path in the routing table of a router. One of the most useful tools that a network administrator has at his disposal in order to help him manage his network is the Simple Network Management Protocol (SNMP).

1.2.1 Simple Network Management Protocol (SNMP)

The Simple Network Management Protocol (SNMP) is an application layer protocol that facilitates the exchange of management information between network devices. This information refers to the configuration and the status of those devices. SNMP is the de facto protocol for network management and is part of the Transmission Control Protocol/Internet Protocol (TCP/IP) stack. In Fig. 1.1 below is shown a brief overview of Internet protocols and SNMPs position in the stack [Ros94].

SNMP is very successful because it requires little code to develop, so it is easy for vendors to implement in their products. By using the SNMP protocol, network managers can detect and solve various problems occurring in a network, control the network's efficiency and performance and easily produce a scheme for increasing network performance [Cis06].

There have been developed three versions of SNMP. These are SNMP version 1 (SNMPv1), SNMP version 2 (SNMPv2) and SNMP version 3 (SNMPv3). The first two versions have many features in common but SNMPv2 is enhanced with additional protocol operations. The Internet Engineering Steering Group (IESG) approved as a full Internet standard the SNMPv3 specifications in March 2002. The SNMPv3 specifications provide additional security and remote configuration functionalities to the previous SNMP [Sys]. Fig. 1.2, shows a simple representation of a network utilising the SNMP [Cis06].

1.2.2 The Basic Components of SNMP

An SNMP-managed network consists of three key components: managed devices, agents, and network management systems (NMSs).

4

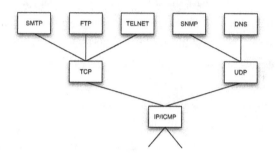

Figure 1.1: SNMP is an application layer protocol

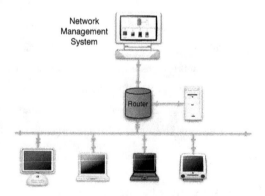

Figure 1.2: A basic network managed by SNMP

Managed Devices

A managed device is a network node that contains an SNMP agent and is attached to a managed network. Managed devices collect and store management information (from and to the Management Information Base (MIB) discussed later in Section 1.2.2) that the NMS can access using the SNMP [Cis06]. They can be classified into three categories [Ros94]:

- A host system, such as mainframe, workstation, printer

- A router system

- A media device, such as bridge, hub or network analyser

Agent

An agent is the software for network management running in a managed device. An agent has local knowledge of management information and converts that information into a form that SNMP can understand [Cis06].

Network Management System

An NMS runs applications that monitor and control managed devices. An NMS provides the processing power and memory resources required for network management. One or more NMSs must exist on any managed network. Figure 1.3 illustrates how these three components can exchange information [Cis06]:

Management Information Base (MIB)

The MIB defines a collection of information that is organized in a hierarchical manner. It is comprised of managed objects that can be identified by object identifiers and are accessed using Abstract Syntax Notation One (ASN.1). By using a network management protocol, such as SNMP, it is possible to access the MIB database [Cis06].

1.2.3 SNMP Basic Commands

Every managed device has an agent, as was previously mentioned, that holds network management information. NMS can monitor and control this information using four basic SNMP commands: read, write, trap, and traversal operations [Cis06].

The read command (snmpget request) is used by an NMS to monitor the managed devices by reading the managed information maintained in them.

The write command (snmpset request) is used by an NMS to control the managed devices by changing the managed information maintained in them.

The management system uses traversal operations to determine the type of information a managed device supports and to gather information from variable tables, such as a routing table.

Trap is the only message sent by an agent on its own initiative. It is used to asynchronously report suspicious events that may demand further attention to the management station (for example a link going down).

1.3 Network Performance Monitoring

Network performance measurement constitutes an important and extensive part of the general network management field. The aim of network performance monitoring is to monitor, measure, analyse, report and control how various network components perform currently or in some instance in the past. These components can be either specific hosts or even an end-to-end route inside the network's infrastructure [KR03].

Network performance monitoring provides statistics and characteristics of the monitored network that are very useful and essential for the network manager, engineers who try to provide network services and researchers who test new applications over the network. With careful examination of the information collected using network monitoring, network managers can find out the shortcomings of the monitored network. For example, they can locate where a bottleneck exists or evaluate the percent of a link's utilisation.

Network administrators who have the task of performance monitoring, will have a lot of difficulties in spotting and preventing network problems. The important key in performance monitoring is the experience one has gained from the mistakes [Tan03].

For enhancing the performance of a network, a loop is employed that includes the following steps [Tan03]:

- Measurement of relevant network performance parameters.

- Processing of those parameters in order to understand the problem.

- Changing a network performance parameter or network topology.

The above loop is repeated until all the problems are solved or there are no more possible changes that would result in better performance.

1.3.1   Background and Immediate Monitoring

Network performance monitoring can be divided into two techniques depending on the point of time that a network is monitored. Background monitoring observes how the network was behaving in a past time instance or period of time, being days, weeks or months. Immediate monitoring simply provides a current snapshot of the network characteristics and conditions [Ben05].

Immediate monitoring is useful for determining the amount of network resources that an application or an end user is able to deploy. Moreover, immediate monitoring detects current problems in the network infrastructure, characterises them (i.e. host down, over-utilisation of link, etc.) and estimates their impact on the rest of the network [Ben05].

Background monitoring is useful when investigating a past situation and for detecting potential or actual network problems. The performance data may exhibit some trends that indicate a possible problem in the near future. Those trends, in the short term, appear insignificant or may not even be detected by a network administrator. Thus, they do not attract the necessary attention leading to the identification of the cause of a problem in the network. Background monitoring gives a solution to this issue by providing long term information about the performance data, making the trend noticeable by the administrator [Ben05].

1.3.2 Active And Passive Monitoring

Network performance monitoring techniques can be divided into passive and active monitoring. In the passive monitoring technique, the network traffic can be observed by monitoring devices but cannot be altered in any way. The conclusions regarding the network performance are made based on the information garnered. That information may not be sufficient enough to let the administrator derive conclusions.

On the other hand, active monitoring involves injecting small data packets in the network traffic for the sole purpose of producing and collecting the required information in order to measure specific parameters of the network.

The advantage of active monitoring is that the injected data packet is controlled and can be modified in order to measure the required network performance information. Thus, many results are produced faster in comparison to the passive monitoring technique. The disadvantage of active monitoring is that the network load is increased by the addition of the injected test packets [SL93].

The active method of monitoring is more suitable for high data rate networks, where the addition of some load in the network does not cause problems with the latency of packets. However, this is not true in a low data rate network where the bandwidth is needed for the efficient transfer of the packets [SL93].

1.3.3 Challenges Of Network Monitoring

There are two reasons why monitoring a network can be challenging. First of all, most networks are heterogeneous, which means that there can be many possibilities for incompatible devices from different vendors to be part of the same network. The second reason is the usually large size of networks. Particularly, the largest network in the world, the Internet, spans most countries around the world. It is reasonable to understand that detecting problems between computers at different sites is much more difficult than if the computers were on the same site [Com99].

It is interesting to note that severe failures in the network are the ones that can easily be detected and corrected. Such failures affect all devices connected to that network, making it easy to pinpoint the source of the problem. However, in the case of intermittent failures, the receiver rejects flawed packets by using the checksum or the CRC. Thus, the sender retransmits the packet, which may arrive at the destination without any interference. So from the users point of view, everything seems working properly. The point is "Because protocols accommodate packet loss, intermittent hardware or software failures can be difficult to detect and isolate." [Com99]

1.4 Network Performance Metrics

In this section, some of the most important network performance metrics, commonly used in research groups, are defined. This is necessary in order to have a universal understanding of the statistics and characteristics that are being measured in any monitored network.

1.4.1 Total Nodal Delay

A journey of a packet starts from the source host, passes a series of nodes and ends in the destination host. When a packet travels from one host to the next host along the journey path, it experiences various types of delays. The most important of these are the nodal processing delay, queuing delay, transmission delay and propagation delay. All of these delays when combined give as a result the total nodal delay, which is the delay at a single router (Fig. 1.4). A description of these delays is presented in the following paragraphs [KR03].

Processing Delay

This delay consists of the time taken for an electronic device in the network, such as, a router, switch, bridge or hub, to examine the packet header and determine where to direct the packet. Moreover, this delay may also include other factors, such as the bit-level error checksum. It is often negligible because of fast CPUs and special-purpose hardware. However, it strongly

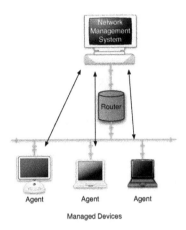

Figure 1.3: Communication between NMS and managed devices

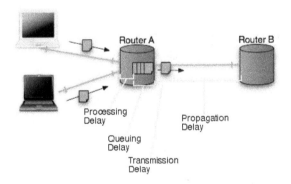

Figure 1.4: Total nodal delay at Router A

affects a router's maximum throughput, which is the maximum packet transmission rate. Processing delay may also be found in literature as Switching Delay named after the time it takes for a device to switch a packet [KR03].

Queuing Delay

This delay refers to the delay that a packet experiences while waiting to be transmitted by a router, or another routing device. The queuing delay of a packet depends on the number of packets that have already arrived and queued waiting to be serviced. There are various algorithms trying to provide a fair queuing system [KR03].

Transmission Delay

Transmission delay, also known as access delay, is the time needed to transmit all of the packet's bits into the link. Practically, transmission delay is on the order of microseconds to milliseconds [KR03].

Propagation Delay

Propagation delay refers to the time needed for a packet to be propagated along some physical medium, be it wire, fibre or even through air. The propagation delay depends on and is one of the characteristics of the physical medium. It is also proportional to the distance spanned [KR03].

1.4.2 End-to-end Delay

As was described above the total nodal delay refers to the delay in one router. The end-to-end delay is essentially the accumulation of nodal delays along the route from the source to the destination. In order to measure end-to-end delay, external clock sources (such as the Global Positioning System

(GPS)) are required for the synchronisation of the source and destination [Tas01, KR03].

As a matter of fact, a network often experiences asymmetric routing. This means that the respective delay encountered by outward-bound packets and returned packets is different [San01]. End-to-end delay provides the delay measurement for a specific path without regarding the delay that a packet experiences while returning to the source [Tas01].

1.4.3 Round Trip Time (RTT)

In contrast to end-to-end delay, round trip time takes into consideration the whole amount of time required for a test packet, usually an ICMP packet, to traverse the network from the source to the destination and return back to the source. In this case there is no need for timing synchronisation because the source clock records the transmission and the reception time. In most applications, it is the RTT that is of most interest because of the focus on the two-way communication between the source and the destination [Tas01, San01].

1.4.4 Jitter

Jitter is the variability of end-to-end delays of packets within the same packet stream. This variability is caused because of the random queuing delays in the routers. The result is a fluctuation in the duration of time from the moment a packet is transmitted up to the moment it is received by the next router. Jitter, or instantaneous packet delay variation as described by the Internet Engineering Task Force (IETF) is a parameter for characterising a network. In real time applications, such as videoconference, it is really important to eliminate the existence of jitter. Otherwise, jitter can result in unintelligible audio or video performance [KR03].

1.4.5 Throughput

Throughput refers to the rate at which data can be sent through the network or a section of the network. In other words, it describes the amount of data that can be sent through the transmission link. It is generally measured in bits per second (or Kilobits/sec, Megabits/sec, etc.). Bandwidth is another term that is often used to describe throughput. Strictly speaking, bandwidth is the throughput capability of the underlying hardware device. Due to the fact that a user cannot send data with a rate faster than that of the hardware's throughput capability, bandwidth is considered to be an upper bound of the throughput [Com99, San01].

Even though throughput and delay are two different measurements of a network, they are closely related. When the traffic access rate of a network is higher than the throughput of the transmission link, congestion occurs on the network. This leads to packets being queued whilst waiting to be serviced. It is obvious that the longer the queuing time the lower the network performance will be [Com99].

Per Flow Application Throughput

This metric measures the throughput for a particular application between specific hosts. It is based on measurements of the actual data exchanged between the two hosts [Tas01].

Aggregate Network Throughput

This metric measures the aggregated throughput within a network between the source host and the destination host. "This may measure the current utilisation as a rate (volume/time) or as a proportion of the total capability within the path across the network." [Li]

1.4.6 Packet Loss / Errors

If a packet arrives in a router device and finds a full queue, then it cannot be stored in the queue and the router will have to drop it. This means that the packet is lost and will not reach it's destination. There are other factors that can lead to packet loss, such as the lack of acknowledgement from the receiver [Li]. In such cases, the hardware and software protocols deal with this problem and trigger the retransmission of the lost packet. The method, with which packet loss is dealt with, depends on the transport protocols (TCP, UDP) and the specific application that generates the packets [KR03, Tas01].

1.4.7 Link Utilisation

The link utilisation metric indicates how much of the throughput of a link is utilised over a specific period of time. For practical reasons, the utilisation should remain under a specific limit, for example 75%; otherwise the response time of the system will increase rapidly as the link utilisation approaches the maximum value [Con02]. The utilisation (U) of the network is calculated using the following expression:

$$U = \frac{total\,bytes\,accepted\,during\,the\,interval\,(including\,overhead)}{theoretical\,max.\,throughput\,for\,that\,interval} * 100\%$$

1.5   Contribution

The performance monitoring and measurement of communication networks is an increasingly important area as demands on and threats to such networks increase. Monitored network data allows network managers and operators to gain valuable insight into the health and status of a network, and if interpreted correctly, can assist in planning upgrades and remedial action to keep the network operating in a near optimum manner.

Whilst such data is useful for real-time analysis, there is often a need to post-process historical network performance data. Such analysis is useful if ongoing long-term problems or if more detailed analysis of a previous situation needs investigation. Storage of the monitored data then becomes a serious issue as network monitoring activities generate significant quantities of data.

Compression of monitored performance data is an attractive option to reduce long-term storage requirements. However, selection of a suitable compression mechanism is a non-trivial activity. Conventionally, lossless compression algorithms have been utilised for this purpose, however it is generally accepted that higher compression ratios are achievable using lossy algorithms. These of course cannot support perfect regeneration of the original data. However, if the important and significant elements of the original data are preserved, lossy compression becomes attractive.

The work described in this book considers this issue and proposes the use of the Wavelet Transform as a first step in the compression of a time-series of delay or utilisation measurements. Using the Wavelet Transform in the manner described in the book allows useful further compression to be obtained over competing lossless algorithms, whilst providing controlled degradation of the signal. The degradation ensures that the important characteristics of the source data are retained and allows later analysis of the measurement data to be implemented efficiently. As far as the author knows this is the first work to propose a *controlled* lossy compression for computer network *measurements* in an *on-line system*.

Further, Wavelet Transformation has the additional benefit of detecting events or sudden changes in network performance measurements through suitable analysis of the derived wavelet domain coefficients. These sudden changes in the measurements are reflections of network performance changes which may occur due to change of load in the network, fault, or planned alterations in the network infrastructure.

The ability to increase the efficiency of storage of network data through intelligent mechanisms is an important, novel and significant contribution to many network management activities.

1.6   Overview

This book is organised in the following way:

Chapter 2 presents important monitoring tools and reviewing several major projects on performance monitoring. In this chapter the project that is closely associated with the work of this book is presented. The challenges of the project and the goals of this work are described.

Chapter 3 discusses the theory of transform based compression techniques. The wavelet analysis is described in detail as it is one of the fundamental tools used in this work. A progressive introduction to the Fast Wavelet transform is presented and the advantages of wavelets against other transforms are explained.

Chapter 4 presents the general operation flow of the compression scheme.

Two threshold estimation methods and two threshold application techniques are presented. The normalisation and run length encoding steps of the operation flow are also explained.

Chapter 5 mainly presents experiments that focus on fine tuning the parameters of the compression scheme. Specifically, it compares the performance of two thresholding methods and examines which one performs better. The results of the selected method are compared against a lossless technique. The two threshold application methods are also compared. An examination of the window size is also presented.

Chapter 6 is divided into five sections. In the first three sections eight different wavelets are compared for their potential to achieve high compression ratios and to preserve the energy, the scaling behaviour and the quality of the analysed signals after their reconstruction. The fourth section is focused on examining the preservation of the long range dependence characteristic. Finally, the on-line implementation of the algorithm and its results are also presented and discussed in the fifth section.

Chapter 7 introduces a different approach to network measurement compression that allows fine tuning of the reconstruction quality in terms of PSNR. The algorithm is based on the Embedded Zero-tree Wavelet algorithm. In this algorithm the PSNR of the reconstructed signal is examined and if it does not meet the specified PSNR value then the compression scheme adds more detail on the reconstructed signal.

Chapter 8 presents an automated tool that uses wavelets to adapt to the time varying environment of a network and detect any abrupt changes that are included in the measurements taken from the examined network. The proposed algorithm uses the coefficients from the wavelet decomposition step of the compression scheme in order to detect abrupt changes. Results are

19

also presented showing the performance of the algorithm.

Chapter 9 provides a summarised conclusion of the aim and results of this work covering all the proposed algorithms. It also discusses a possible solution for a faster implementation of the compression scheme.

1.7 Summary

The performance monitoring and measurement of communication networks is an increasingly important area as demands on and threats to such networks increase. In this chapter, the most popular protocol for network management is introduced followed by discussions about background and immediate monitoring, active and passive monitoring and challenges of monitoring. Important network performance metrics like the total nodal delay, round trip time, jitter, throughput, packet loss and others are defined and discussed.

CHAPTER 2

Related Work in Performance Monitoring

2.1 Introduction

The topic of network performance monitoring is of great importance and most network research groups have developed their own means of measuring the performance of networks. In this chapter, some of the most well known tools available for network measurements are introduced. Their objective is to measure common network performance metrics, such as RTT, bandwidth, packet loss etc.

The rest of this chapter is focused on bigger projects from various known researchers in the network measurement area, such as CAIDA, RIPE, NLANR. Many research groups have developed and tested their own Network Measurement Infrastructure (NMI) [fIDACb]. An NMI can be described as a system responsible for monitoring the network, measuring statistics describing the performance of that network, providing a large number of storage devices in order to store the measured information and finally presenting the information to the network administrator. [CZUM99, CM99, fIDACb] have comparison tables for some of the most significant NMIs.

Finally, the UKLight initiative is introduced in this chapter. The UK-Light initiative is a 10 Gbps, high capacity research network facility that interconnects several other continental research networks with JANET, the UK's research and educational network. The MASTS (Measurement and Analysis in all Scales of Time and Space) project has been initiated to provide a performance monitoring system for the UKLight. As will be discussed in Section 2.4, the work in this book is part of the MASTS project.

2.2   Performance Monitoring Tools

2.2.1   Ping

The ping program, written by Mike Muuss, is a diagnostic tool for examining whether another host is reachable or not. It makes use of the ICMP echo request and echo reply messages transmitted between the source and destination hosts. Additionally, it measures the round-trip time (RTT) to a host, the time-to-live (TTL) value and gives an idea about the distance of the host [Ste94].

The ping program also supports the IP Record Route (RR) option. This enables all the IP addresses of the routers that have routed the ICMP packet to be logged in the options filed of the packet. When the destination host is reached, the list of IP addresses is copied to the ICMP echo reply packet. Similarly, the IP addresses of the return path routers are also logged in the reply packet. However, due to some limitations described in [Ste94] the task

22

of recording the IP addresses of the path is left for the traceroute program.

2.2.2 Traceroute

The traceroute program is written by Van Jacobson and can be used to find the route that an IP packet follows from a source node to a destination node. The route is described by the IP addresses of the routers that have handled the IP packet. Another use of traceroute is detecting route changes. The traceroute tool takes advantage of the 8-bit TTL field in the header of an IP packet. As the IP packet travels through routers, every router decreases the TTL value by one. When the value of TTL reaches one, the host should not forward the packet but, instead, drop it [Ste94].

The key of traceroute's concept is the ICMP TTL-expired reply that a router sends to the sender when it drops a packet. This message indicates that the packet reached its "end of life" but also holds the IP address of the router [DTRS01]. Thus, traceroute sends IP packets with increasing TTL value each time, and collects the IP addresses of the routers until the packet reaches its final destination [Ste94].

2.2.3 Iperf

The Iperf utility was motivated by the need of a modern tool to measure TCP and UDP throughput. Additionally, Iperf measures jitter, packet loss and reports the maximum segment size (MSS) and the maximum transmission unit (MTU) [TQD+].

2.2.4 cflowd

The cflowd utility is used for capturing, storing and analysing network traffic flows from Cisco's NetFlow switching method. The amount of data stored is adjustable and can vary from a few hundreds of Kbytes to many hundreds of Mbytes per router in a time period of one day. This tool can be applied in many areas such as link capacity planning, traffic trend analysis and workload characterisation [fIDACa, Tas01].

2.2.5 MRTG

The Multi Router Traffic Grapher (MRTG) is a tool written in C and Perl and its development was motivated by the need to monitor traffic load on network-links. MRTG uses the SNMP in order to collect information about the traffic counters of routers, system load, login sessions and any other SNMP variable. MRTG presents the collected information in a user-friendly way. It produces HTML web pages with PNG images that give a live update of the measured metrics [Oet].

2.2.6 Pathchar TReno

The pathchar tool measures bandwidth, propagation and queue delay and packet loss rate in a per hop basis. The TReno tool focuses only on measuring bulk transfer throughput [MM].

2.3 Performance Monitoring Projects

2.3.1 NIMI

The National Internet Measurement Infrastructure (NIMI) is an NMI for the Internet developed by Vern Paxson. It is motivated by the need to monitor the global Internet. It's monitoring technique is based on active measurements between monitoring probes strategically positioned throughout the network. These probes measure the properties of Internet paths and clouds [PMAM98].

NIMI's main purpose is to detect and diagnose faults in networks extending to the full Internet scale. NIMI has a scalable architecture in the sense of being able to incorporate any third party tool for measurement purposes. It currently supports traceroute, poip (Poisson Ping) and Treno and can measure vital metrics of a network such as throughput, one-way delay and packet loss [PMAM98].

2.3.2 Surveyor

Surveyor is another example of an NMI deployed in U.S., Canada, Europe and New Zeland and is based on work done in IETF IP Performance Monitoring (IPPM) [CZUM99]. It makes active end-to-end performance measurements of the Internet. It is used to make measurements regarding one-way end-to-end delay, packet loss and routing information. There are also modules developed for the Surveyor project dedicated in analysing the garnered performance data [Tas01].

The Surveyor project relies on dedicated PC's running Unix and being placed on distant monitoring sites. Global Positioning System (GPS) antennas are used in order to synchronise the time clocks between the monitors

[CM99]. Surveyor transmits its test-packets between the monitors in a Poisson distribution in order to avoid synchronisation of the test data with the actual network data [San01].

2.3.3 RIPE NCC Test Traffic Measurements

Similarly to the Surveyor project, the Test Traffic Measurements (TTM) project also uses active monitoring, synchronisation using GPS antennas, and Poisson distribution of test packets in order to measure network metrics. TTM was developed with the purpose of independently measuring connectivity parameters. The metrics that TTM can measure include: one-way end-to-end delay, packet loss, route information, bandwidth and jitter. This information can be made available to the user in the form of plots showing results of the last days or months [CZUM99, Eur].

2.3.4 PingER

The Ping End-to-end Reporting (PingER) project is an active monitoring infrastructure that uses ICMP packets to make network measurements. It measures round-trip time, packet loss, variability of round-trip time and the lack of response from hosts. In comparison to Surveyor, PingER is lighter, uses less bandwidth and requires less storage. It is suitable for remote hosts with poor quality connections [CZUM99, Tas01].

2.3.5 AMP

The Active Measurement Program (AMP) is a part of NLANRs (National Laboratory for Applied Network Research) project for developing a network measurement infrastructure. It uses active monitoring and measures RTT, topology characteristics and packet loss. This project was motivated by the need to understand the performance of high-speed networks from the users point of view [fANR, San01].

2.3.6 Skitter

The Skitter project is supported by CAIDA (Co-operative Association for Internet Data Analysis) and actively monitors the Internet in order to garner information about the topology and the performance. More precisely, it measures the path between a source and many destinations (forward IP path) by increasing the TTL value of each packets IP header. Additionally, Skitter measures the RTT and records the changes in routing paths [fIDACc].

2.3.7 Comparing Performance Monitoring Projects

It would be interesting to give a comparison between the six performance monitoring projects discussed above. Table 2.1 shows a comparison for various characteristics and metrics for each described network performance monitoring project [CZUM99]. It should be noted that the unknown fields in the table are represented with a question mark.

The above projects should be regarded as complementary as their goals are not the same and they monitor different paths spanning different countries. Because the Surveyor makes the most frequent sampling of measurements it gathers the most data. On the other hand, PingER has the smallest data storage rate. PingER has also the longest collected historical data and spans most countries in comparison to the other projects [CZUM99]. None of the projects above deal with the issue of intelligently compressing and storing vast amount of measurements.

27

Project	Surveyor	RIPE	PingER	AMP	Skitter	NIMI
Metric	1 way delay	1 way delay	RTT	RTT	topology	1 way delay
	packet loss	packet loss	packet loss	packet loss	performance	packet loss
	routing	route	RTT variability	topology		throughput
		bandwidth	no response			
		jitter				
Synchronisation	GPS	GPS	NTP	NTP	NTP	other
Locations	US, CA, EU, NZ	EU, IL, US	32 counties	US, NZ, NO	Asia, CA, UK, US	?
Data start	1997	1998	1995	1999	1998	?
Pairs	1000	1024	1200	4600	35000	?
Data storage	38MB	2Mbytes	0.6MB	1.3MB	?	?

Table 2.1: Comparison of Monitoring Projects

2.4 UKLight and the MASTS Project

2.4.1 Introduction to UKLight

This work described in this book is motivated by the need to measure the performance of high-speed communication networks of the future and particularly of the UKLight experimental network. The UKLight initiative is a 10 Gbps, high capacity research network facility that interconnects several other continental research networks with JANET, the UK's research and educational network. These other continental research networks include, STARLIGHT in the USA (Chicago), NETHERLIGHT in the Netherlands (Amsterdam), CANARIE (Canadian academic network), CERN in Geneva, and NorthernLIGHT of Nordic countries.

The purpose of the UKLight venture is to create an international experimental testbed, giving the researchers around the world the opportunity to access facilities located to different continents, such as, for example, Internet2 via STARLight, and participate in Grid-nature projects where huge data sets are transferred between distant sites. Additionally, researchers can deploy in the testbed altered and enhanced versions of transport and network layer protocols and examine their impact on the network.

UKLight is expected to be a platform with a diverse mixture of traffic and data flow. It will be an important asset for the Academic community, attracting researchers from various fields that would like to practice on a high data rate, high bandwidth future network. For instance, researchers interested in networking technologies as well as application development requiring high flow rates, would have a platform on which to run their experiments and evaluate relatively new protocols and technologies (e.g. Reliable multicast, IPv6, MPLS). Additionally, researchers can deploy in the testbed altered and enhanced versions of the transport and network layer protocols and examine their impact on the network. Thus, a need is created that requires a tool for evaluating the efficiency of those experiments and their impact on the whole network [Sac].

Figure 2.1 below presents the infrastructure of the international components of the UKLight facility.

2.4.2   The MASTS project

The performance monitoring and measurement of communication networks is an increasingly important area as demands on and threats to such networks increase. Monitored network data allows network managers and operators to gain valuable insight into the health and status of a network, and if interpreted correctly, can assist in planning upgrades and remedial action to keep the network operating in a near optimum manner.

The MASTS (Measurement and Analysis in all Scales of Time and Space) project has been initiated to provide a performance monitoring system for the UKLight. The objective of the monitoring system is to acquire, store and analyse vast amounts of network data produced by a highly distributed network, over a long period of time. The term "network data" refers to data flows, network performance metrics (see 1.4) and topological information and will be recorded at various time scales, ranging from fractions of second, up to years [Sac].

The recorded information will be made available to the community around the world through a web service utilising a management interface. Thus, it will be possible to have knowledge of any user defined network performance measurement at any moment in the past up to the current moment.

Whilst such measured data is useful for real-time analysis, there is often

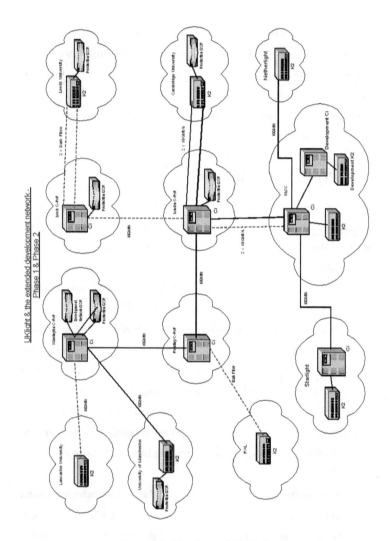

Figure 2.1: Topology of UKLight

a need to post-process historical network performance data. Such analysis is useful if ongoing long-term problems or if more detailed analysis of a previous situation needs investigation. Storage of the monitored data then becomes a serious issue as network monitoring activities generate significant quantities of data.

2.4.3 Challenges

At the heart of the MASTS project is the need to derive an efficient method of on-line analysis and reduction in order to archive and store the enormous amount of monitored traffic. The real challenge, however, is to be able to preserve the statistical characteristics of the sampled data. Satisfying this need is useful not only for administrators but also for researchers who run their experiments on the monitored network. The researchers would like to know how their experiments affect the network's behaviour in terms of utilisation, delay, packet loss, data rate etc. Such signals are derived from packet level information and can be represented as a time series process. As an example, Figure 2.2 shows a data rate signal. The y-axis indicates the data rate in Mbps and the x-axis the sampling period of time.

There are two main challenges in the MASTS project that should be considered. The first is the high speeds of traffic transport that UKLight is capable of delivering. As was mentioned before, UKLight is a high-speed network that reaches the speed of 10 Gbps. The second is the duration of the network's active status, during which the traffic is recorded. This duration spans a large number of years, which is a long period of time. These characteristics of the UKLight network produce such a vast amount of information that it is practically inefficient to be stored as it requires a large number of storage devices. This itself significantly increases the cost for measuring

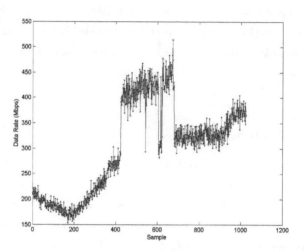

Figure 2.2: An example of a data rate signal

high-speed networks [Sac]. Table 2.2 below shows an approximation of the
time required to fill 1 TB of storage by assuming an average packet length
of 500 Bytes and header length 64 Bytes per captured packet for a 10 Gbps
link. It should be noted that only the headers are stored and the payload
is dropped. The number of 64 bytes of headers was estimated by assuming
preservation of the transport layer (UDP or TCP), the network layer (IP)
and of the physical layer header including the maximum possible number of
virtual local area networks a packet could transit.

Compression of monitored performance data is an attractive option to
reduce long-term storage requirements. However, selection of a suitable
compression mechanism is a non-trivial activity. Conventionally, lossless
compression algorithms have been utilised for this purpose, however it is
generally accepted that higher compression ratios are achievable using lossy

Network Utilization	Packets/sec	Bytes/sec	Time to fill 1 TB
100%	2.5×10^6	160×10^6	1.74 hrs
80%	2×10^6	128×10^6	2.2 hrs
60%	1.5×10^6	96×10^6	2.9 hrs
40%	1.0×10^6	64×10^6	4.34 hrs
20%	5.0×10^5	32×10^6	8.68 hrs
10%	2.5×10^5	16×10^6	17.4 hrs

Table 2.2: Estimated filling time for 1 TB. 500 Bytes assumed packet length

algorithms. These of course cannot support perfect regeneration of the original data. However, if the important and significant elements of the original data are preserved, lossy compression becomes attractive.

As was mentioned before, the measured metrics can be represented as time series processes. Thus, these signals can be analysed and compressed with a signal analysis technique. The work described in this book considers the above issues and proposes the use of the Wavelet Transform as a first step in the compression of a time-series of delay and utilisation measurements.

Other compression techniques were initially considered before choosing wavelet transform such as the Discrete Cosine Transform (DCT) and fractal analysis. Early experiments with the DCT did not provide satisfactory results in comparison to the wavelet transform. This happens because DCT lacks the adaptability of wavelets onto different types of signals and does not preserve the scaling characteristics of the measurements as accurately as wavelets.

On the other hand fractals would be perfect for compressing self-similar measurements. However the results will not be adequate when the analysing window is not similar to the examined segment of the measured signal as it would require many parameters to describe non self-similar measurements. Wavelet transform can achieve adaptability and high compression ratios in both cases, even when the signal is self similar even when it is not

Using the Wavelet Transform allows useful further compression to be obtained over competing lossless algorithms, whilst preserving statistical characteristics of the signals and providing an adaptive degradation of the signal. The degradation ensures that the important characteristics of the source data are retained. Furthermore, the use of the Wavelet Transform allows later analysis of the measurement data to be implemented efficiently. Some examples of further analysis may be estimating the long range dependency and the energy of the measured signal.

2.4.4 Goals of Lossy Compression

As was previously mentioned, monitoring high-speed communication networks produces a large amount of data over a long period of time. Storing all this network performance information is practically inefficient as a large amount of storage capacity is required. A possible solution to this problem is to reduce the amount of data or, in other words, apply compression. In the case of lossless compression, the achieved compression ratios are not satisfactory, making the choice of lossy compression mandatory.

The work described in this book examines compression schemes that offer compression ratios which are driven from the need to preserve specific quality and statistical characteristics of the reconstructed signal. Such characteristics are, for example, the PSNR, the scaling behaviour and the long range dependency. Thus, the use of the Wavelet analysis technique offers variable compression ratio between the original and the reconstructed signals depending on the examined signal's frequency characteristics rather than a specified amount of storage capacity.

By applying wavelet analysis techniques on the measured computer network measurements, sharp and unpredictable (sudden) changes in the characteristics of the measured quantity can be detected. Changes that differ from the rest of the signal are considered exceptional and should be preserved.

Later on, in the wavelet domain the information that describes the signal is structured in a more compact format that allows manual or automatic reduction of information in specific frequency bands of the signal. In order to have satisfactory compression ratios, the bigger a change is, the more information should be preserved in order to describe it. On the other hand, if the change is not as significant, less information will be preserved in order to increase the compression ratio.

By adjusting the reduction of information in an automatic and dynamic manner, important features in the original time series are preserved, while "expected" features are subjected to higher reduction of information due to their less significant nature. In that way, interesting events that describe the network performance keep their detail and preserve in a better extent their original characteristics. As a result, it is easier for the administrator or a researcher that runs experiments on the test network to draw conclusions regarding the effect of their experiments on the network with higher accuracy.

Furthermore, apart from high compression ratios and good reconstruction signal quality, several factors of the compressed signal should be investigated in order to determine the effect of compression on them. The following list shows the goals of compression including statistical and quality aspects that should be preserved. It should be noted that the list is not an exhaustive list and as our understanding of the computer networks improve other parameters could be required in the future and might not be preserved.

1. Offer high compression ratios

2. Quality characteristics

   - Preserve sudden changes: peaks and dips
   - High PSNR - Low Mean Square Error

3. Statistical Characteristics

   - Preserve Long Range Dependence
   - Preserve Energy
   - Preserve Mean and standard deviation

Spikes and overall quality

When times of very high network usage occur, spikes in the data traces are reported. On a public network, such spikes would be of considerable importance as they indicate periods of high load and their further investigation may indicate if changes to the network are required. On a research network such as UKLight, analysis of the spikes may indicate what impact a particular experiment has had on a given network path. Preservation of these spikes for later analysis is therefore of great importance.

The quality of the reconstruction signals was compared with the original by using the PSNR value calculated from

$$PSNR = 10 * log\left(\frac{MAX^2}{MSE}\right) \tag{2.1}$$

where MAX is the maximum value of the original signal and MSE is the mean square error calculated from

$$MSE = \frac{1}{N} \sum_{i=0}^{N-1} |x_i - \bar{x}_i|^2 \tag{2.2}$$

where x_i is the ith sample from the original signal, $\bar{x}_i$ is the ith sample of the reconstructed signal and N is the total number of samples.

It should be noted that PSNR comparisons are valid only when comparing the same signal. Comparisons between different signals are not valid as the maximum value of each signal may be different.

Long Range Dependence

Leland et al., with their well-known publication in 1994 [LTWW94], showed that Ethernet LAN traffic does not follow the Poisson model as was commonly assumed. They proved that Ethernet LAN traffic is self-similar i.e. the network traffic is bursty across a wide range of time scales.

Self-similarity can be described as the property of a data set to look or behave the same when viewed at different time or space scales [AKR]. Some self-similar processes are given in [Ros96]. Self-similarity of network traffic depends on the network utilisation level and is described by the Hurst parameter [LTWW94].

The long-range dependence (LRD) is one of the properties that self-similar processes have and it is also described by the Hurst parameter [Ros96]. It is a way to measure the memory of a process or, in other words, how correlated distant events of a process are. By examining the autocorrelation function (ACF) of a LRD process we can find out how similar that process is with shifted versions of itself. For LRD data, the ACF follows a power-law behaviour (i.e. slowly decaying) whereas for short-range dependence data the ACF decays exponentially (i.e. quickly decaying) [AKR].

In recent years, many studies have been conducted observing the self-similarity and long-range dependence phenomena in various networking contexts like ATM, VBR video and the world-wide-web (WWW) [CB97, WPRT01,

RW00, ST99, FGWK98, VKMV00]. Many studies have concluded that LRD significantly increases queuing delays and leads to packet loss [ENW96]. Furthermore, LRD and self-similarity are important concepts for network modelling, traffic synthesis, and queue analysis [RRB01, LTWW94]. The above issues have led the network community to become involved in identifying and view the Hurst parameter as a key concept in signal analysis. Thus, its preservation after applying any compression is an important issue.

Energy

[AV98] have first introduced a plot, called the *energy function plot*, for determining the range of scales of a process that exhibit self-similarity and for estimating the Hurst parameter for stationary or stationary-increment data. They used a statistic known as the *energy function* E_j which indicates the average energy of the arrival process contained at scale j and is defined by [AV98]:

$$E_j = \frac{1}{N_j} \sum_k |d_{j,k}|^2, \qquad j = 1, 2, ..., n \qquad (2.3)$$

where N_j is the number of wavelet ("detail") coefficients at scale j, $d_{j,k}$ is the kth detail coefficient at scale j and k takes values from 1 up to the maximum number of coefficients at scale j (i.e. it is an index for each coefficient).

The energy plot can be generated by plotting the $log(E_j)$ against the scale j from finer to coarser scales. Intuitively, this plot illustrates the scaling behaviour of the underlying time series (such as a traffic arrival process) at different time-scales.

This tool has been used from many researchers [VV06, SB04, RNV06, RRB07] for evaluating their traffic models with respect to the correct reproduction of the scaling structure of the modelled traffic. By comparing the burstiness of the synthesised and original traffic at a variety of scales, researchers can evaluate how closely their model matches the correlation structure of the modelled network. Such kind of research is important for resource planning, router design, queue management and flow classification among others.

[FGHW99] have demonstrated that highly regular or periodic structures in a time series reveal themselves in the wavelet domain as small value coefficients. Additionally, they show how the energy plot can reveal such periodicities as "dips" in the graph.

As a simple example, consider the periodic time series X that has length of 1024 and its values are the series $0, 0, 1, 1, 1, 1, 0, 0$ repeated 128 times. By applying the DWT and using the discrete Haar wavelet transform functions described later in Section 3.3.5, we observe that periodic patterns appear at all scales except from scale $j = 2$ which is irregular (see Fig. 2.3).

Table 2.3 shows the initial time series $X_{0,k}$ at the finest scale $j = 0$ and the subsequent values of the aggregate and difference processes (approximation and detail coefficients).

In [HFW01], authors have used the energy function to passively infer and extract network path problems using IP packet traces recorded off a network link . Problems such as sudden load changes, congestion and route changes have an effect in the time scale associated with the dominant round-trip time (RTT). Because, the dominant RTT is a periodic (regular) process, it is revealed as dips in the energy function plot.

In [Jar04] the author follows a similar approach and tries to detect congestion in an aggregate traffic signal generated by more than one TCP sources. The work demonstrates how changes in the RTT of a network path (associated with the congestion) result in the redistribution of energy amongst the

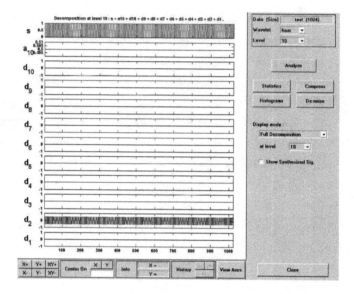

Figure 2.3: Regularities in a time series reveal as small coefficients in the wavelet domain

wavelet coefficients at different frequency bands. Furthermore, proposes a method to distinguish between high and low levels of packet loss.

2.4.5 CoMo

Continuous Monitoring (CoMo) is supported by Intel's Research laboratory at Cambridge. The projects leader is Gianluca Iannaccone. CoMo is the most probable candidate of a "building block" on which an open NMI for the UKLight will be designed. It is a passive monitoring platform developed for the purpose of monitoring network links at high speeds (up to 10 Gbps) and replying to real-time queries regarding network statistics.

X 0	X 1	d 1	X 2	d 2	X 3	d 3	X 4	d 4
0	0	0	1	-1	1.4142	0	2	0
0	1.4142	0	1	1	1.4142	0	2	0
1	1.4142	0	1	-1	1.4142	0	2	0
1	0	0	1	1	1.4142	0	2	0
1	0	0	1	-1	1.4142	0	2	0
1	1.4142	0	1	1	1.4142	0	2	0
0	1.4142	0	1	-1	1.4142	0	2	0
0	0	0	1	1	1.4142	0	2	0
0	0	0	1	-1	1.4142	0	2	0
0	1.4142	0	1	1	1.4142	0	2	0
1	1.4142	0	1	-1	1.4142	0	2	0
1	0	0	1	1	1.4142	0	2	0
1	0	0	1	-1	1.4142	0	2	0
1	1.4142	0	1	1	1.4142	0	2	0
0	1.4142	0	1	-1	1.4142	0	2	0
0	0	0	1	1	1.4142	0	2	0

Table 2.3: Original time series and approximation and detail coefficients at scales 1, 2, 3 and 4. X_0 is the original time series, X_i and d_i are the approximation and detail coefficients at scale i

There are three challenges that CoMo's design has to deal with. First of all, the platform should allow computation of any kind of metric on the incoming traffic flow. Secondly, privacy and security issues should be taken into consideration. Lastly, the platform should be able to cope with very fast data rates and still be robust without experiencing black-out periods.

CoMo's architecture is open, flexible and can accommodate various third party software modules for measuring and querying the traffic metrics and statistics. A module can be regarded as a combination of a filter and a process. The filter selects only specific packets and then the process is applied to these packets to compute a metric [IDM$^+$04].

2.5   Summary

In this chapter, performance monitoring tools are presented that measure performance metrics, such as round-trip time, route taken, bandwidth and packet loss. These tools are used in bigger projects that try to measure different performance characteristics of large scale networks. Some of the greatest players in the network performance monitoring field are presented.

The purpose of the UKLight venture is introduced and described as a means to create an international experimental testbed, giving the researchers around the world the opportunity to access facilities located to different continents. Researchers can deploy in the testbed altered and enhanced versions of the transport and network layer protocols and examine their impact on the network.

The researchers would like to know how their experiments affect the network's behaviour in terms of utilisation, delay, packet loss, data rate etc. Such signals are derived from packet level information and can be represented as a time series process.

Using the Wavelet Transform allows useful further compression to be obtained over competing lossless algorithms, whilst preserving statistical characteristics of the signals (mean, standard deviation, long range dependence, energy) and providing an adaptive degradation of the signal.

By adjusting the reduction of information in an automatic and dynamic manner, important features in the original time series are preserved, while "expected" features are subjected to higher reduction of information due to their less significant nature.

In the following chapter, an overview of transformed based data compression methods is presented followed by a detailed description of the Wavelet Analysis, implementation in practice and its advantages.

CHAPTER 3

Transform Based Compression

3.1 Introduction

There have been many techniques developed for data compression, but a specific family of those techniques, named transform compression, are considered to be more efficient and valuable. The reason is that transforming time series signals into another domain (usually associated with the frequency domain), reconstructs the signal information in a more compact form from which it is easier to identify the most relevant and characteristic attributes of the signal. Transform compression is based on the following key principle: When any type of transform (for example Fourier or Wavelet) is applied on an examined signal, the resulting data values do not carry any longer the same amount of information [Smi06].

The low frequency components of a signal provide a better representation for the original signal than the high frequency components. An example follows to make that easier to comprehend: a human voice signal would still be recognisable and understandable if the high frequencies were removed. However, this is not true if the low frequencies were removed.

Thus, by removing most of the high frequency components of the signal, a very good compression with negligible degradation in quality is achieved [Smi06]. However, further research is required on evaluating the effect of the compression on the various statistics that were described in the previous Section 2.4.4.

There have been various types of transforms developed. Some well-known examples of transform compression techniques are the Fourier transform, the short-time Fourier transform and the Discrete Cosine Transform (DCT). Recently (early 90's), there has been interest in the Wavelet transform in many areas, which is being discussed later in this Chapter [Smi06].

3.2 Fourier and Short Time Fourier Analysis

The Fourier analysis is one of the most frequently used tools for signal analysis. It simply decomposes a signal into a collection of sinusoids of different frequencies. In other words, Fourier analysis transforms the signal from the time domain to the frequency domain, thus revealing information about the signal that is hidden in the time domain [MMOP04, Sri03].

Fourier analysis is not considered to be an appropriate tool for signals that exhibit non-stationary characteristics such as drifts, trends and abrupt changes. The main drawback with Fourier analysis is that it does not provide time information, making it impossible to tell when particular frequencies are present (see Fig. 3.1) [MMOP04, Sri03].

In an effort to correct this shortcoming, the Short-Time Fourier Analysis (STFA) uses a windowing technique to divide the whole signal into small portions assuming them to be stationary. Later, the Fourier Transform is applied on each of these portions. STFA reveals both at what time periods and with which frequencies an event occurs. However, the accuracy and precision of this information is limited by the size of the window [MMOP04, Sri03].

The Heisenberg uncertainty principle states that it is not possible to know which *frequencies* exist at which time *instance* but it is possible to know the frequency *bands* that exist in a time *period* [Sri03]. Consequently, in STFA when the window is small, the time resolution is high but the frequency resolution is poor (see Fig. 3.2 a). When the window is large, the time resolution is poor but the frequency resolution is high (see Fig. 3.2 b). A varying window size would give the ability of calibrating the level of resolution for either time or frequency [MMOP04].

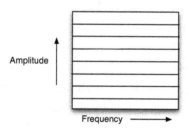

Figure 3.1: Amplitude-Frequency Tiling for Fourier Analysis

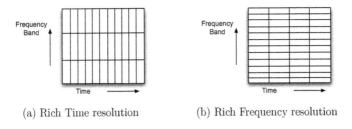

(a) Rich Time resolution   (b) Rich Frequency resolution

Figure 3.2: Tiling for the Short Time Fourier analysis.

3.3 Wavelet Analysis

3.3.1 Introduction to Wavelets and Wavelet Analysis

In a similar way to the STFA, wavelet analysis is a windowing technique but with varying window size. Usually, Wavelet analysis uses a long window at low frequencies and a short window at high frequencies (Fig. 3.3). In other words, at low frequencies, the time resolution is poor but the frequency resolution is high. At high frequencies, the time resolution is high but the frequency resolution is poor. Thus, a high frequency can be located in time domain more precisely than a low frequency. On the other hand, a low frequency can be located in the frequency domain more precisely than a high frequency [Sri03].

A wavelet for the wavelet analysis is the equivalent of the sine wave for the Fourier analysis. "A wavelet is a waveform of effectively limited duration that has an average value of zero" [MMOP04]. In comparison to a sine wave, a wavelet is irregular, sharp and of limited size rather than predictable, smooth and infinite.

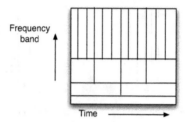

Figure 3.3: Time-Frequency Tiling for Wavelet Analysis

3.3.2 Continuous Wavelet Transform

In a similar way to the Continuous Fourier transform, we can define the Continuous Wavelet Transform (CWT) as "the sum over all time of the signal multiplied by scaled, shifted versions of the wavelet function ψ". This sum results in a set of wavelet coefficients that are a function of scale and position [MMOP04].

$$C_{scale,shift} = \int_{-\infty}^{\infty} f(t) \times \psi(scale, shift, t)dt \qquad (3.1)$$

In order to produce the CWT coefficients, the following steps take place:

1. A wavelet is chosen and is compared against the analysed signal at the starting point.

2. A coefficient is generated that indicates how similar the wavelet is with the corresponding part of the examined signal. The higher the value of the coefficient, the higher the resemblance between the two signals.

3. The wavelet is shifted to the right and steps 1 and 2 are performed until the whole signal is examined.

4. The wavelet is scaled and steps 1-3 are repeated.

5. Steps 1-4 are repeated for each scale.

When we multiply each of the coefficients with the specified scaled and shifted version of the wavelet we produce the constituent wavelet components of the original signal [MMOP04].

Scaling and shifting

When we are referring to the scale of a wavelet we mean how much stretched or compressed the wavelet is. The higher the scale of the wavelet, the more stretched the wavelet is. The more stretched a wavelet is (higher scale, higher level of decomposition), the longer the compared signal's section will be and thus the cruder the measured features.

On the other hand, the more compact the wavelet is (lower scale, lower level of decomposition), the shorter the signal's section will be and thus the more detailed the features [MMOP04]. Shifting a wavelet simply means delaying the wavelet's starting point. Figures 3.4 and 3.5 below (taken from [MMOP04]) explain graphically the two concepts.

Figure 3.4: Scaled versions of wavelet. [MMOP04]

3.3.3   Discrete Wavelet Transfrom

In order to make the Continuous Wavelet Transform more efficient but preserve it as accurate, the Discrete Wavelet Transform (DWT) is used. The

Wavelet function
$\psi(t)$

Shifted wavelet function
$\psi(t-k)$

Figure 3.5: Shifted versions of wavelet

difference from the CWT is that only scales and positions based on powers of two are used.

DWT maps the information of a time series $x(t)$ into approximation $a_x(J,k)$ and detail $d_x(j,k)$ coefficients in the wavelet domain. In these j is the scale level and takes values from $[1 \ldots J]$, where 1 is the lowest, most detailed scale, and J is the crudest; k is the position of the wavelet in relation to the signal.

$$x(t) \rightarrow \{\{a_x(J,k)\}, \{d_x(j,k), j = 1, 2, \ldots, J\}\} \tag{3.2}$$

The approximation coefficients are defined as the inner product of signal $x(t)$ with shifted and scaled versions of the scaling (a.k.a. father) function $\phi(t)$. For this reason the approximation coefficients are also called scaling coefficients.

Similarly, the detail coefficients are defined as the inner product of the signal $x(t)$ with shifted and scaled versions of the wavelet (a.k.a. mother) function $\psi(t)$. Thus, the detail coefficients are also referred to as *wavelet* coefficients.

$$a_x(j,k) = \langle x | \phi_{j,k} \rangle \tag{3.3}$$

$$d_x(j,k) = \langle x | \psi_{j,k} \rangle \tag{3.4}$$

The scaled and shifted versions of the scaling and wavelet functions can be defined as

$$\phi_{j,k}(t) = 2^{-\frac{j}{2}} \phi_0(2^{-j}t - k) \tag{3.5}$$

$$\psi_{j,k}(t) = 2^{-\frac{j}{2}} \psi_0(2^{-j}t - k) \tag{3.6}$$

The scaling and the wavelet function definitions depend on the choice of DWT, which can be orthogonal (Haar, Daubechies, Coiflets, Symmlets), semi-orthogonal or bi-orthogonal (Spline).

3.3.4 Multi-resolution Analysis

Assuming a time series $x(t)$, the Multi-resolution analysis at scale J decomposes the information in signal x into a collection of a series of detail signals, ranging from the finest (lowest) scale up to scale J (highest), and a low-resolution approximation signal at scale J. Fig. 3.6, taken from [MMOP04] shows the multi-resolution analysis including the approximation and detail signals at each scale.

$$x(t) = approx_J(t) + \sum_{j=1}^{j=J} detail_j(t) \tag{3.7}$$

The approximation signal, $approx_J(t)$ is generated by convolution of the approximation coefficients (equation 3.3) and the scaling function $\phi(t)$. The approximation signal is the coarsest approximation of signal x that can occur during the wavelet analysis meaning that the scaling function behaves as a low-pass filter.

The collection of detail signals $\sum_{j=1}^{j=J} detail_j(t)$ is generated similarly by convolution of the detail coefficients (equation 3.4) with the wavelet function

52

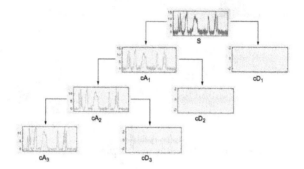

Figure 3.6: Multi-resolution Analysis. cA is the approximation and cD is the detail signal for scales 1, 2 and 3. [MMOP04]

$\psi(t)$ at each scale. The detail signal at each scale is essentially the difference between two scales j and $j + 1$. In other words, the wavelet function behaves as a band-pass filter, which looks like a wave and therefore the name "wavelet".

Thus, equation 3.7 can be written as

$$x(t) = \sum_k a_x(J, k)\phi_{J,k}(t) + \sum_{j=1}^{j=J} \sum_k d_x(j, k)\psi_{j,k}(t) \qquad (3.8)$$

As was mentioned in Section 3.3.1 wavelets have a mean value of zero and another characteristic property is the number of vanishing moments N, which can be defined as

$$\int t^k \psi(t) d(t) = 0 \qquad k = 0, 1, \ldots, N - 1 \qquad (3.9)$$

If the average value of $\int t^k \psi(t) d(t)$ is zero for $k = 0, 1, 2, \ldots, N - 1$, then the wavelet has N vanishing moments and polynomials of degree $N - 1$ are suppressed by this wavelet. In general a wavelet becomes smoother and more regular as the degree of vanishing moments is increased [MMOP04].

53

3.3.5 Multi-resolution Analysis: The Haar wavelet approach

The Discrete Haar wavelet analysis transforms a given signal $S_{0,k}$ (0 is the finest scale and k is the number of samples $[0, 1, \ldots, k]$) into $k/2$ approximation (scaling) and $k/2$ detail (wavelet) coefficients. The approximation coefficients represent the smoothed version of the signal (low frequency bands), while the detail coefficients represent the detailed version (high frequency bands).

The basic idea of wavelet analysis is that an average (with an unusual normalisation factor, see equations 3.10) of two samples of signal S at scale j produces an approximation coefficient at the next higher scale $j + 1$. The difference between those samples produces a detail coefficient at scale $j + 1$.

Thus, for a specific scale, approximation coefficients are associated with the averages, whereas detail coefficients represent the change of averages. In the case of the simplest wavelet function, Haar, for the first and second sample, this can be expressed as:

$$\alpha_{j+1}[0] = \frac{S_j[0] + S_j[1]}{\sqrt{2}} \qquad d_{j+1}[0] = \frac{S_j[0] - S_j[1]}{\sqrt{2}} \tag{3.10}$$

and because α coefficients are the aggregate signal at higher scales, the above equations can be generalized as:

$$S_{1,k} = \frac{1}{\sqrt{2}}(S_{0,2k} + S_{0,2k+1}) \qquad d_{1,k} = \frac{1}{\sqrt{2}}(S_{0,2k} - S_{0,2k+1}) \tag{3.11}$$

Wavelet Analysis can be used as a Multi-resolution Signal Decomposition (MSD) tool, decomposing a signal into scales of varying time and frequency resolution.

Initially, the first level (or scale) of decomposition of the multi-resolution analysis takes place (Fig. 3.7). The same process can be applied again on the previously produced $(k/2)$ approximation coefficients yielding $k/4$ detail and approximation coefficients and so on for higher scales. The total group of detail coefficients from scale 1 up to J and the approximation coefficients at scale J compose the wavelet decomposition tree at scale J.

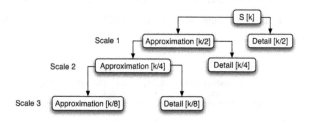

Figure 3.7: Multi-Resolution Signal Decomposition

3.4 The Fast Wavelet Transform: Filterbanks

3.4.1 Introduction

Because of the above advantages that wavelet analysis offers, it has been decided to implement the Fast Wavelet Transform (FWT) as a module for the CoMo platform (discussed in Section 2.4.5) in order to perform data reduction.

In 1988, Mallat [Mal98] developed the Fast Wavelet Transform (FWT) algorithm that became well known in the signal processing community as a two channel subband coder using conjugate filters or quadrature mirror filters (QMF) [MMOP04]. The Mallat algorithm utilises a filter bank of direct form structure. The Mallat algorithm is divided into the decomposition and the reconstruction parts which are explained in the following paragraphs [Sri03].

3.4.2   Wavelet Decomposition

The decomposition (or analysis) process takes the original signal of length n, and passes it through the analysis filter bank (AFB) in order to produce the wavelet coefficients of the first level decomposition. The maximum level of decomposition is $log_2 n$. For a multi-level decomposition, the approximation coefficients are recursively passed as input in the AFB algorithm as shown in Fig. 3.8. The wavelet decomposition coefficients are obtained by concatenating the approximation and detail coefficients, starting from the last decomposition level [Sri03, CL, MMOP04].

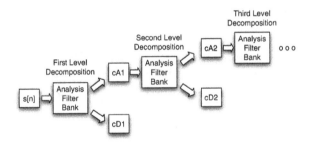

Figure 3.8: Multi-level Decomposition Block Diagram

The analysis filter bank is of a direct form structure and is pictured in Fig. 3.9.

The original signal of n samples is first convolved with the low and high pass filters, each one of length N. As a result, signals X and Z are produced. Due to the convolution, their length is equal to $n + N - 1$. Those two signals are later down-sampled in order to get the approximation and detail

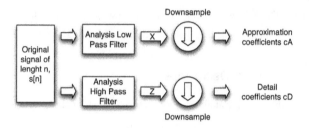

Figure 3.9: Analysis Filter Bank Block Diagram

coefficients, cA and cD respectively. Both groups of coefficients have length equal to lc (see equation 3.12) [Sri03, CL, MMOP04].

$$lc = \left\lfloor \frac{(n + N - 1)}{2} \right\rfloor \tag{3.12}$$

3.4.3 Wavelet Reconstruction

The reconstruction (or synthesis) process reconstructs the signal from the coefficients. The process is exactly the reverse of that followed in the decomposition phase. The approximation and detail coefficients of the last decomposition level j are passed through the synthesis filter bank (SFB). The result is the approximation coefficients of level $j - 1$.

For a multi-level reconstruction, the approximation and detail coefficients of each level, starting from the last level, are recursively passed through the SFB as shown in Fig. 3.10. The synthesis filter bank is shown in Fig. 3.11 [Sri03, CL, MMOP04].

The coefficients are first up-sampled and the resulting signals L and M have size of $(2 * lc + 1)$. The latter signals are then convolved with the coefficients of the low-pass and high-pass synthesis filters. The signals A' and D' have size equal to $2 * lc + 1 + N - 1$ i.e. $2 * lc + N$. It is notable that

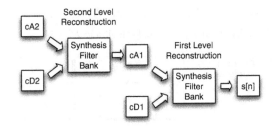

Figure 3.10: Multi-level Reconstruction Block Diagram

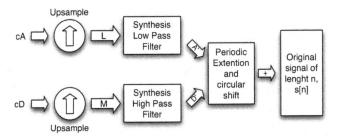

Figure 3.11: Synthesis Filter Bank Block Diagram

there is an excess of N samples, where N is the length of each filter, for both A' and D' [Sri03, CL, MMOP04].

In order to avoid this excessive length, a procedure called periodic extension is followed. In this procedure, the last N coefficients are removed and added to the first N coefficients, thus eliminating the excessive length [CL].

Another problem that arises is that by adding A' and D' to reproduce the original signal, what actually is produced is a circular translated version of the original signal. In other words, in the resulting signal, the last samples of the original signal appear in the beginning and the initial samples appear in the end (see Fig. 3.12). However, the number of samples that is shifted is known and equals to the length of each filter. Thus, there is a work around to this problem by circularly shifting both A' and D' [CL].

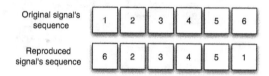

Figure 3.12: Circular shift process

3.4.4 Choosing filters

Unfortunately, the down-sampling process during the decomposition, introduces an amount of distortion to the signal known as aliasing. In order to avoid the aliasing effect, the QMF coefficients of the analysis and synthesis phases have to be closely related. Apart from determining the quality of the reconstructed signal, the filters also determine the shape of the wavelet used in the wavelet transform.

Reference [MMOP04] presents a scheme that takes as an input a wavelet and calculates the four filter coefficients required in both phases of the transform. The wavelet, also referred to as a scaling filter, is a Finite Impulse Response (FIR) low-pass filter of $sum = 1$ and $norm = \frac{1}{\sqrt{2}}$

The scheme (Fig. 3.13) first calculates the low-pass synthesis (Lo_R) filter by dividing the wavelet coefficients by $norm(S) = \frac{1}{\sqrt{2}}$. The low-pass analysis (Lo_D) filter is the reverse of the low-pass synthesis. The high-pass synthesis filter (Hi_R) is the reverse of the Lo_R but with the opposite sign for the even indexed coefficients. Lastly, the high-pass analysis filter (Hi_D) is the reverse of the Hi_R. The above can be summarised in Fig. 3.13.

In the proposed on-line implementation of the algorithm (described in

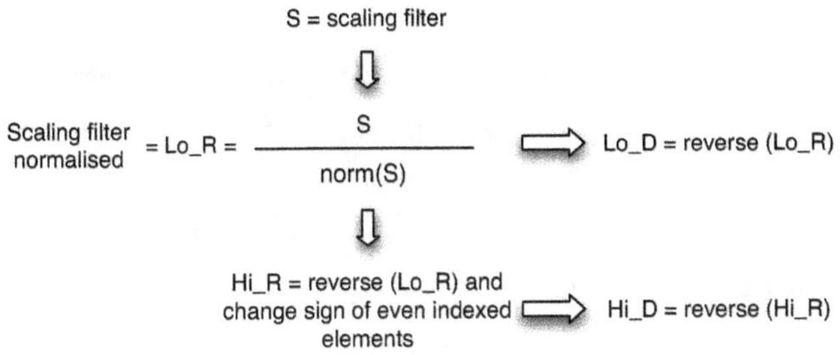

S = scaling filter

⇩

$$\text{Scaling filter normalised} = \text{Lo\_R} = \frac{S}{\text{norm}(S)}$$ ⟹ Lo_D = reverse (Lo_R)

⇩

Hi_R = reverse (Lo_R) and change sign of even indexed elements ⟹ Hi_D = reverse (Hi_R)

Figure 3.13: Computing the QMF coefficients from the scaling filter

Chapter 6.6), the four filters were derived from the Haar wavelet as it performed similarly, if not better, than the other wavelets. The QMF coefficients for the Haar wavelet can be seen in Fig. 3.14 below.

Low-pass Analysis Filter	=	0.7071 0.7071	Low-pass Synthesis Filter	= 0.7071 0.7071
High-pass Analysis Filter	=	-0.7071 0.7071	High-pass Synthesis Filter	= 0.7071 -0.7071

Figure 3.14: QMF coefficients

3.5 Advantages of wavelets and their use in Computer Networks

In contrast with other signal analysis techniques that use a constant window size to analyse a section of a signal (for example DCT, STFT), wavelet analysis has the benefit of varying the window size. This means that wavelets can efficiently trade time resolution for frequency resolution and vice versa. For this reason, wavelets can adapt to various time-scales and perform local analysis. In simple words, wavelets can reveal both the forest and the trees [MMOP04] [Agb96].

Wavelets have the ability to detect characteristics of non-stationary signals due to their finite nature that describes local features better than say sinusoids. Non-stationary signals are stochastic signals whose statistical properties change with time. A lot of research in network traffic analysis shows that packet switched data traffic patterns are statistically self-similar. Self-similar processes are by definition non-stationary [ABF+02] [LTWW94].

One characteristic advantage of wavelets is the ability to tell when a particular event has taken place. This happens because in contrast with the amplitude-frequency plot in Fourier transform, wavelets provide a frequency-time plot.

So far, wavelets have been generally used to detect network performance problems. They have been applied to traffic rate signals in order to infer the time scale associated with the dominant RTT through the examination of the energy function of the detail coefficients ([HFW01]). They have also been used for de-noising one-way delay signals in order to detect shared congestion between different flows in [KKS+04]. [BKPR02] shows that wavelet filters are quite effective at exposing the details and characteristics of ambient and anomalous traffic. [KRV04a, KRV04b] analyse the correlation of destination IP addresses of outgoing traffic at an egress router. Based on statistical historical margins, estimated after using wavelet analysis, sudden changes are detected.

As far as the author is aware there is no other research at the time of writing this book for using wavelet analysis to offer controlled lossy compression on computer network measurements.

3.6 Summary

In this chapter the Wavelet analysis was introduced, starting from how the Wavelet Transform begun as a concept and the reasons that it was developed. The theoretical background is discussed, covering the Continuous and Discrete Wavelet Analysis and the concept of Multi-resolution analysis. Particularly the Haar algorithm is described in detail as it will be the one that will mainly be used in the following methodologies.

Furthermore, the Fast Wavelet Transform is explained as it is the algorithm that is actually implemented in this work. All the steps of the algorithm are covered in order for the reader to be able to reproduce the algorithm while understanding the insights and pitfalls. Details are also given regarding how to generate the mathematical values of the Haar filter in order to be used in the Fast Wavelet Transform.

Finally, the advantages of Wavelets over other transform based methods are presented along with a review of the different areas that wavelets have been used in the computer network field.

CHAPTER 4

Methodology

4.1 Introduction

Wavelet analysis is not a compression tool but a transformation to a domain that provides a different view of the data that is more eligible to compression than the original data itself. The connection between lossy compression and denoising has been discussed in several papers, for example in [CYV00] and references therein. In this work, denoising techniques are used in order to achieve compression.

Fig. 4.1 shows the flow chart of the main algorithm for analysis and compression of each examined signal and the reverse process for reconstructing each signal. First the signal is transformed into the wavelet domain (see Section 3.4) where the threshold is calculated (see section 4.2) and applied (see Section 4.3) on the wavelet coefficients. Then, the thresholded coefficients are normalised (see Section 4.4) so that each coefficient can be stored in 1 byte and finally run length encoding is applied (see Section 4.5).

4.2 Thresholding

As was mentioned in Section 3.3.5, detail coefficients actually reveal the changes of the average. In other words, detail coefficients with large magnitude represent significant changes in the original signal. These large magnitude detail coefficients need to be preserved because they represent important characteristics of the signal and they should be kept in order to preserve the quality of the signal [CYV00, KGC02].

On the other hand, many of the wavelet coefficients produced from the wavelet analysis have an absolute value close to zero. These small coefficients are probably attributable to small variations of the signal and contain a small percentage of the signal's total energy. These small coefficients can be discarded without a significant loss in the quality of the signal and more importantly of the interesting features. Thus, a threshold is required below which all coefficients will be discarded.

4.2.1 The Birge Massart Threshold

Even though a lot of research has been done in selecting a threshold [MMOP04, KGC02, DJ94, Don95, CYV00, DJ95, DJKP95], most of it is focused on recovering signals that have been corrupted by additive Gaussian noise. In this chapter two threshold selection schemes that depend on the values of the wavelet coefficients are deployed and compared.

The first scheme that is examined is proposed by Birge and Massart and has become a popular threshold selection technique used widely in image and

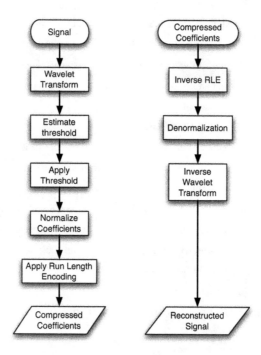

Figure 4.1: Operation flow chart

speech compression [MMOP04]. The scheme depends on three parameters:

1. The level of decomposition J

2. A positive constant M

3. A sparsity parameter α

This scheme keeps all approximation coefficients at the level of decomposition J. At each level i only the n_i largest coefficients are kept. n_i is estimated by the formula:

$$n_i = \frac{M}{(J+2-i)^\alpha} \tag{4.1}$$

Usually, α takes the value 1.5 for compression and M depends on how scarcely the wavelet coefficients are spread and on the number L of approximation coefficients in the coarsest level (Table 4.1). For highly scarcely spread coefficients, M becomes equal to the number L. For low scarcely spread coefficients M becomes twice the number L.

Scarce	M value
High	L
Medium	1.5*L
Low	2*L

Table 4.1: M depends on how scarce the coefficients are spread.

In our experiments, for delay signals the high scarcity option of the Birge Massart algorithm was used. For data rate the low scarcity was more appropriate as more coefficients were required for more precise reconstruction.

4.2.2 The Kaur Gupta Threshold

The second of the examined threshold selection techniques was recently proposed by [GK02]. It is an adaptive thresholding technique that is calculated from the absolute value of the wavelet coefficients. This scheme is not based on signal denoising but rather tries to statistically identify significant coefficients. Specifically, the standard deviation (σ) and mean (μ) of the absolute value of non-zero detail coefficients are first calculated. If the standard deviation is larger than the mean, then the threshold is set to two times the mean ($2*\mu$), otherwise it is equal to the mean minus the standard deviation ($\mu - \sigma$). Thus, the threshold, T, can be expressed mathematically as:

$$T = \begin{cases} 2*\mu, & if \sigma > \mu \\ \mu - \sigma, & if \sigma \leq \mu \end{cases} \qquad (4.2)$$

4.3 Applying the Threshold

The hard and soft thresholding techniques are two of the most common ways of applying a threshold. In both cases coefficients with absolute value smaller than the threshold are set to zero. With the hard threshold all coefficients with absolute value larger than the chosen threshold are kept intact, while with the soft threshold, positive coefficients are reduced and negative coefficients increased by the value of the threshold. In other words coefficients that have an absolute value larger than the threshold are shrunk towards zero, thus naming this method shrinkage as described in [Don95]. The hard and soft threshold functions are given below in equations 4.3 and 4.4 and are illustrated in Fig. 4.2 for threshold T=0.5.

$$f_{hard}(x) = \begin{cases} x, & if \quad |x| \geq T \\ 0, & otherwise \end{cases} \qquad (4.3)$$

$$f_{soft}(x) = \begin{cases} x - T, & if \quad x > 0 \quad and \, |x| \geq T \\ 0, & if \quad |x| < T \\ x + T, & if \quad x < 0 \quad and \, |x| \geq T \end{cases} \qquad (4.4)$$

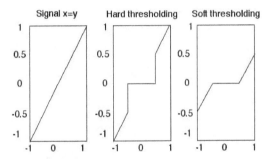

Figure 4.2: Hard and soft thresholding functions for threshold T=0.5

Depending on the examined signal and the application, the threshold technique has to be chosen carefully. [KGC02, YV04] use soft thresholding to avoid abrupt artefacts produced from the discontinuity of hard thresholding (see Fig. 4.2) and to provide smoothness to the reconstructed signal.

[DS98] recommend using the hard thresholding technique rather than the soft technique as it gives less MSE. The hard thresholding method performs better as it offers a more precise reconstruction of signals that contain abrupt changes but also retains a large amount of the original signal energy. In Section 5.5 the quality of reconstructed signals between hard and soft thresholds are compared.

4.4 Normalisation

In order to improve the way that data is stored, normalisation of the coefficients needs to take place. The aim is to use just 8 bits to store each
coefficient. However, with an 8 bit variable only 256 values can be stored
(values $0 \ldots 255$) or 127 values (i.e. 2^7 bits) saving one bit for the sign of the
wavelet coefficient. Thus, first the coefficient values have to be normalised
using the following formula:

$$norm(x) = round\Big(\frac{x - min}{max - min} * scaling\, factor\Big) \qquad (4.5)$$

where x is a coefficient, min is the minimum value that appears in the array
of coefficients and max the maximum. The scaling factor in this case is 127,
which is the maximum value of a signed number that can be stored in 1
byte. In order to avoid the detail coefficients being skewed by the larger
values of the approximation coefficients, the normalisation process is applied
separately for the detail and for the approximation coefficients.

4.5 Run Length Encoding

The simplest version of the run length encoding (RLE) algorithm replaces a
sequentially repetitive symbol with the symbol itself followed by a number
that indicates how many times the symbol should be repeated. However,
this simple version of RLE expands single symbols into a pair of symbol-run
length.

In order to avoid this shortcoming, a more sophisticated RLE implementation utilises a run length that is used only for symbols that appear more
than 2 times. This method has beneficial effect only for symbols that appear
3 or more times. However, the RLE limitation persists for symbols that ap-

pear sequentially for just two instances and expand into symbol-symbol-run length triples. This version of RLE is preferred to the previous one, because the probability of a symbol appearing twice is significantly lower than appearing once.

4.6 Examined Data

For the off-line experiments (Chapter 5) and the wavelet comparison investigation (Chapter 6), thirty delay and thirty data rate signals of 1024 points were used.

The delay signals were measured on a research test bed. Traffic generators were used to emulate a time of day profile similar to that of a commercial network. Seven of the delay signals (signals 1, 2, 4, 14, 16, 17, 21) are smooth with sudden discrete bursts spread over the data, signal 10 is a very bursty delay signal and the rest include some burstiness along with spikes [San01].

The data rate signals are from a real commercial network that generates around 25 TB of data per day and has data rates between 500 Mbps and 1.4 Gbps. In a window size of 2 seconds 30,000 unique IP addresses may be observed in that network [SP07]. Two data rate signals (signal 1 and 16) include large sudden changes and three other signals include medium size changes (signals 20, 27, 30). The rest of the data rate signals are generally bursty with some having trend upwards and others downwards.

4.7 Discussion of the Operation Flow Chart

In each step of the operation flow chart (Fig. 4.1) there are some technical parameters that should be selected in order to have a complete compression scheme. The technical questions that arise by close examination of the operation flow chart are:

- How large should the captured signal be before it is analysed, transformed and compressed (i.e. which window size is better) ?

- Up to which level of decomposition is it important (in terms of compression ratio and reconstruction quality) to analyse a signal ?

- Which of the two threshold estimation techniques that were presented in this chapter performs better ?

- How does the selected threshold estimation scheme perform against a lossless algorithm ?

- How should the threshold be applied ? Is it the hard threshold method better than the soft threshold or not ?

All the above questions are addressed in Chapter 5 starting by identifying the most powerful threshold selection scheme. The selection of an appropriate threshold is the most crucial step of all operation steps in figure 4.1. No matter how optimum the window size and examination wavelet, the results are not going to be useful if the threshold selection step lacks performance.

In Chapter 6 the author investigates which type of wavelet performs better in terms of preserving the quality characteristics of the reconstructed signal, the energy of the signal, the statistical parameters as defined in 2.4.4 and the offered compression ratio. The Long Range Dependence preservation is also examined.

4.8 Summary

This chapter discusses the main operation followed for the purpose of compressing collected network measurements. All the steps shown in the flow chart in Fig. 4.1 were introduced and explained in each section. Two threshold estimation schemes and two methods of applying the estimated threshold were introduced. In order to take advantage of the applied threshold normalisation and run length encoding steps were used to incur the compression. There are several parameters in each step that need to be specified before having a complete compression scheme. In the next chapter these parameters will be discussed and examined.

CHAPTER 5

Selecting Parameters for the Compression Scheme

5.1 Introduction

This chapter examines the performance of two compression techniques in terms of quality and compression as the level of decomposition increases. The two techniques are the GK and BM methods as described in Chapter 4. First, the performance of quality of reconstruction against compression ratio is examined for both techniques. Later on, the technique that performs better is further examined for compression performance and a comparison is given against bzip2 [Sew08].

Off-line experiments were run with the signals, described in Section 4.6, fed as input to the wavelet thresholding algorithm (Fig. 4.1). Experiments were run on an Intel Core Duo machine at 1.83Ghz and were aimed at producing results regarding the compression ratio (C.R.) and PSNR of the decompressed signal.

In order to examine if the normalisation and RLE steps of the coefficient values in the compression scheme have any negative effect on the error of the reconstructed signal, the same experiments are repeated with and without applying the normalisation and RLE steps. The MSE is calculated for relative comparison between the cases of applying the normalisation and RLE steps and of omitting them.

The results show that for most cases the average error of compression is similar if either normalisation and RLE are applied or not. The only exception happens when the data rate signals are examined with the GK technique at specific scales as will be discussed later in Section 5.3.

MSE is also used to indicate how the error increases with increase of the decomposition level. It's value itself is not of concern, as it does not reveal much about the quality of the reconstructed signal. The quality of the reconstructed signal is compared with the original by using the PSNR value.

In addition to PSNR values, figures are also provided to demonstrate how the decompressed signals compare to the original signals. The error between the original and reconstructed signals is also provided for easier understanding of the magnitude of error.

The effect of the window size is also discussed in this chapter. The window size is the length of the measured signal that needs to be analysed and compressed. In other words the author examines how the compression ratio, the reconstruction error and the window size relate to each other.

Finally, after concluding which method performs better in terms of compression ratio and reconstruction quality the hard and soft threshold application techniques are compared in order to identify which one gives better results.

5.2 Results for the Birge Massart (BM) technique

Fig. 5.1 shows the compression performance and Fig. 5.2 the error of compression with and without the normalisation step for the delay signals with respect to the level of decomposition. As the level of decomposition increases, the number of approximation coefficients decreases and so does the number of kept detail coefficients as can be inferred from equation 4.1.

As a result the MSE and C.R. become very high above level 4, giving an average PSNR of 34.2 dB at level 4. From experimental experience, for both delay and data rate signals, PSNR values less than 35 dB loose some of the important signal characteristics while PSNR values less than 30 dB are not acceptable for such signals. As an example of how low PSNR values affect visually the quality of the reconstructed signal Figure 5.3 and Figure 5.4 are provided. Especially in Figure 5.3, the error (PSNR less than 30 dB) significantly distorts the original signal. Table 5.1 includes PSNR and C.R. values for the first four levels of decomposition where PSNR remains above 30 dB.

Level	L1	L2	L3	L4
PSNR	51.2	43	38.5	34.2
C.R.	5.3	7.9	13.1	22.6

Table 5.1: PSNR and C.R. values for levels 1-4 of decomposition for delay signals with the BM technique.

The first two levels of decomposition give good PSNR values (above 40 dB) and perform very well for almost all signals. Fig. 5.5 shows signal 24, its reconstruction and the error after analysis at level 2. PSNR is 40.3 dB

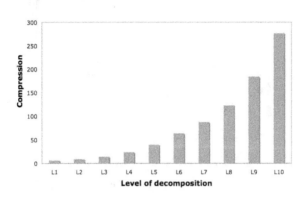

Figure 5.1: Performance of compression for delay signals with BM technique

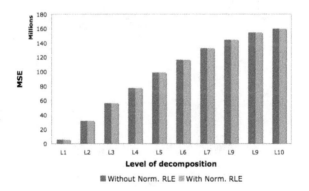

Figure 5.2: Error of compression for delay signals with BM technique

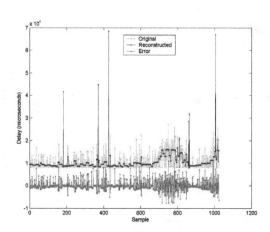

Figure 5.3: Delay signal 29 decomposed at level 4 with the BM method.
PSNR=29 dB

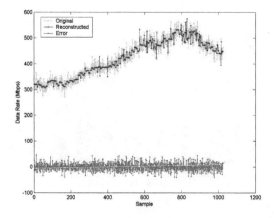

Figure 5.4: Data rate signal 29 decomposed at level 4 with the BM method.
PSNR=31.94 dB

and C.R is 7.59.

Signal 10 of the experiments is the only signal from the delay measurements that is much more bursty than the rest. Due to this fact, it includes many high frequency components and it is the hardest delay signal to compress. The BM technique fails to retain the quality of that signal even at the lowest level of decomposition giving a PSNR of 25.7 dB and C.R. =6 at level 1 (Fig. 5.6). A more suitable algorithm is required for such bursty signals in order to keep more coefficients and perform better in preserving their quality.

Regarding the data rate signals, the performance of compression behaves as in delay signals (Fig. 5.7). The significant increase in error at level 10 (see Fig. 5.8) occurs because the nominator in equation 4.1 is very small which makes the number of kept detail coefficients in each level very small. Compression ratios and PSNR values for the first 5 levels are given in Table 5.2. From level 6 and above the average PSNR values become less than 30 dB and are not included in Table 5.2.

Level	L1	L2	L3	L4	L5
PSNR	51.7	38.4	34.6	32.7	31.6
C.R.	10.3	13.2	20.5	34.2	58.7

Table 5.2: PSNR and C.R. values for levels 1-5 of decomposition for data rate signals with the BM technique.

The BM technique behaves the same in all cases for the data rate signals keeping values of PSNR for all signals in the range range 49 dB to 52.8 dB for level 1 and 35.7 dB to 40.7 in level 2. Fig. 5.9 shows signal 16, its reconstruction with PSNR=40.7 dB and the error after analysis at level 2. The compression ratio is 7.86.

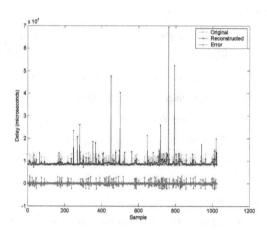

Figure 5.5: Delay signal 24 decomposed at level 2 with the BM method. PSNR=40.3 dB and C.R.=7.59

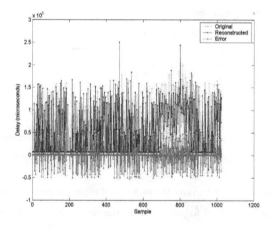

Figure 5.6: Delay signal 10 decomposed at level 1 with the BM method PSNR=25.7 and C.R.=6

79

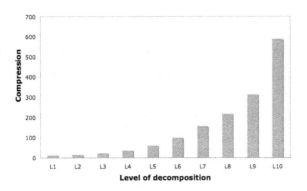

Figure 5.7: Performance of compression for data rate signals with the BM technique

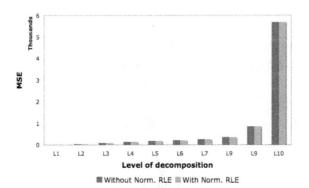

Figure 5.8: Error of compression for data rate signals with the BM technique

5.3 Results for the Gupta Kaur (GK) technique

With the GK algorithm implemented in the C language, for a level-6 wavelet analysis and compression procedure, each signal of 1024 measurements required on average 33 ms to complete. First the results for delay signals using the GK technique are discussed and then the results of data rate signals.

Fig. 5.10 shows the performance of compression and Fig. 5.11 the average MSE of the reconstructed signals over the depth of decomposition. The C.R. begins at 7.5 for level 1 and stabilises around 17 from level 6 and above. The MSE stabilises after level 7. The PSNR and C.R. average values for all levels are shown in Table 5.3.

Fig. 5.12 shows delay signal 30, which is a good representative of most of the delay signals, before and after the compression. Because the two signals are very similar, the error between them is also provided for better judgement (lower line). The signal is decomposed at level 10 and the reconstruction quality is 37.85 dB while the C.R. is 13.7.

In contrast to the BM technique, GK performs very well in keeping the reconstructed quality of signal 10 even at the crudest level. This happens because GK uses the statistical characteristics of the coefficients to determine the number of coefficients that should be kept. Thus, the algorithm is able to adjust to the burstiness of the signal and produce a reconstructed signal with very low error. The results can be seen in Fig. 5.13. PSNR is 44.3 dB and C.R. is 5.65.

In contrast with the delay signals, for the data rate signals there is no significant increase in the compression ratio as the level of decomposition increases (compare Fig. 5.10 with Fig. 5.14). The PSNR and C.R. average

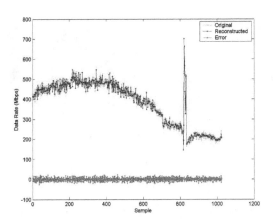

Figure 5.9: Data rate signal 16 decomposed at level 2 with the BM method
PSNR=40.7 dB and C.R.=7.86

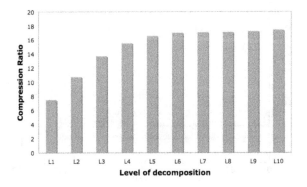

Figure 5.10: Performance of compression for delay signals with the GK technique

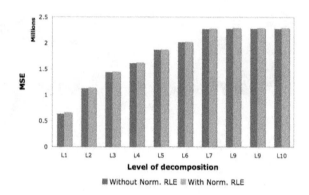

Figure 5.11: Error of compression for delay signals with the GK technique

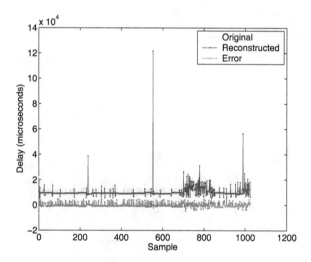

Figure 5.12: Delay signal 30 decomposed at level 10, PSNR= 37.85 dB and
C.R.= 13.7.

Level	L1	L2	L3	L4	L5	**L6**	L7	L8	L9	L10
Min. PSNR	37.0	34.3	33.5	33.1	33.1	**32.8**	32.8	32.8	32.8	32.8
Max. PSNR	54.6	53.1	52.6	51.8	50.9	**50.1**	49.7	48.5	48.5	48.5
Avg. PSNR	44.3	42	41	40.5	40	**39.6**	39.2	39.2	39.2	39.2
C.R.	7.5	10.7	13.6	15.5	16.5	**17**	17	17	17.2	17.4

Table 5.3: PSNR and C.R. Values for Delay Signals After Reconstruction using the GK Algorithm

values for all levels of decomposition for data rate signals are in Table 5.4. The C.R. range is between 10.5 and 11.2 in contrast with the wider range (7.5 - 17.4) for delay signals (see Table 5.3). This happens because data rate signals have a lot of high frequency components that make the GK algorithm to keep a lot of detail coefficients in order to preserve the signal quality.

An interesting implication of the normalisation and RLE steps with the wavelet coefficients of the data rate signals is that the compression performance does not stabilise as happens with the delay signals. In particular, there is a decrease in C.R. after level 5 and a sudden peak at level 10 (Fig. 5.14).

This is because by increasing the level of decomposition in data rate signals, some of the produced coefficients are much larger than the rest of coefficients. In other words the dynamic range of the detail coefficients before the normalisation step is increased. For this reason, after the normalisation step, close values are assigned the same normalised value. This phenomenon happens occasionally across the coefficients exploiting the RLE limitation and producing file sizes that are larger than the files before the RLE step.

At the highest decomposition level, the dynamic range is so large that

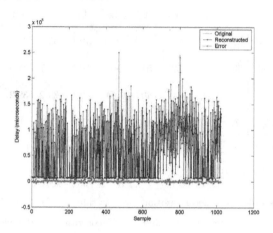

Figure 5.13: Delay signal 10 decomposed at level 10 with GK method, PSNR=44.3 dB and C.R.=5.65

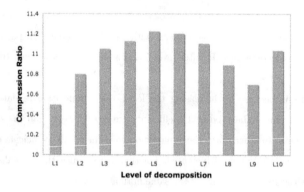

Figure 5.14: Performance of compression for data rate signals with the GK technique

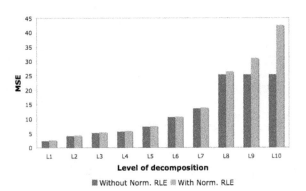

Figure 5.15: Error of compression for data rate signals with the GK technique

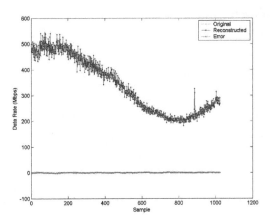

Figure 5.16: Data rate signal 20 decomposed at level 5 with the GK method, PSNR=56.9 dB and C.R.=10.53

Level	L1	L2	L3	L4	**L5**	L6	L7	L8	L9	L10
Min. PSNR	39.0	37.2	36.4	36.4	**35.4**	34.0	34.0	33.2	32.7	32.7
Max. PSNR	58.6	58.1	57.6	58.0	**57.5**	57.2	56.7	55.6	55.0	52.8
Avg. PSNR	56.3	55.6	55.4	55.2	**54.9**	53.4	49	43.9	42.1	39.4
C.R.	10.5	10.8	11	11.1	**11.2**	11.2	11.1	10.9	10.7	11

Table 5.4: PSNR and C.R. for Data Rate Signals After Reconstruction

many detail coefficients normalise to the value of zero (because the denominator in equation 4.5 is very high). In that case the RLE takes advantage of the repeating values but also the MSE increases because of the loss of detail coefficients (Fig. 5.15).

This is the only case for which the normalisation and RLE steps significantly increase the error of the reconstructed signal. However, this is only limited to the last three levels of decomposition for data rate signals(Fig. 5.15).

Fig. 5.16 shows an example of a data rate signal decomposed at level 5 with the GK method. The reconstructed signal has very good quality as it is visually indistinguishable from the original signal and offers PSNR=56.9 dB, very low error and C.R.=10.53.

Fig. 5.17 shows a more interesting case of a data rate signal. This signal includes a spike, which is kept intact after the compression. A characteristic of the GK algorithm is that it detects the spike as a more interesting feature than the rest of the signal. As a result, the algorithms first priority becomes to preserve this characteristic and then comes the rest of the signal.

This actually means that the large coefficients representing the big spike will shift the threshold to higher values, thus, filtering out more smaller magnitude coefficients. This is the reason why PSNR is around 35 dB and there is higher error for the rest of the signal in comparison to signal 20 in Fig. 5.16, which is similarly bursty but with no spike. The high reconstruction error is accompanied by a high C.R.= 26.57.

It should be noted that the RLE encoding outperforms the arithmetic coding (A.C.)(see Section 7.2.5) because there are long sequences of zeroed thresholds. Table 5.5 shows the averaged results between the RLE and arithmetic coding for compressing 30 delay signals. For the first two levels of decomposition the arithmetic coding performs better but after that it looses its advantage.

Encoding	L1	L2	L3	L4	L5	L6	L7	L8	L9	L10
A.C.	10.55	10.82	11.82	12.99	14.3	15.25	15.5	15.81	15.95	16.37
RLE	7.467	10.70	13.64	15.49	16.54	16.98	17.04	17.05	17.18	17.38

Table 5.5: Average values for compression ratio for 30 delay signals for all levels of decomposition with arithmetic encoding and run length encoding

5.4 Comparing the Compression Performance of the GK Algorithm Against bzip2

Fig. 5.18 and Fig. 5.19 compare the C.R. results of the GK wavelet technique at level 10 of decomposition against bzip2. It is interesting to examine the results from the wavelet transform against a non-transform compression technique. The reason bzip2 was chosen was because it is an excellent lossless compression tool and a natural option when no other obvious alternatives exist for compressing network measurements.

Each examined signal is located on the x-axis. The y-axis shows the file size in bytes. On average, for delay signals (Fig. 5.18) the GK method (WT) achieves compression 6.5 times greater than bzip2 with the best score being 11 times and the worst score 2.3 times. For data rate signals (Fig. 5.19) the average compression is 4.7 times greater than bzip2 with the best score being 12 times and the worst 4 times.

5.5   Hard and Soft Threshold Comparisson

In this section a comparison is given between the hard and soft thresholds. Fig. 5.20 shows the average mean square error (MSE) of the reconstructed signals for all decomposition levels. The value of MSE is used only for relative comparison between the hard and the soft thresholding methods. The value itself is not of concern, as it does not reveal much about the quality of the reconstructed signal. Fig. 5.20 shows that as the level of decomposition increases, the two graphs increasingly diverge. Clearly the hard thresholding method affects the reconstructed signal to a lower extent than the soft method.

This happens because hard thresholding is discontinuous and has the characteristic of maintaining abrupt changes during the reconstruction and preserving the energy of the original signal [DS98]. Furthermore, the modifying nature of soft thresholding is not suitable for such signals, especially as the decomposition level increases, because wavelet analysis is a recursive process and an error in an early stage perpetuates to the later stages.

Fig. 5.21 shows the performance of compression over the depth of decomposition for both hard and soft threshold filtering. On average, for level 10, hard thresholding compresses the original file 17.3 times, while soft thresh-

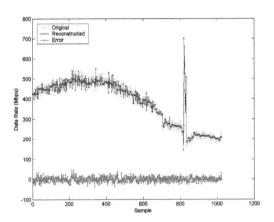

Figure 5.17: Data rate signal 16 decomposed at level 5 with the GK method, PSNR=35.4 dB and C.R.=26.57

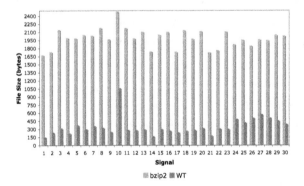

Figure 5.18: Compression performance of the wavelet algorithm (level 10 decomposition) against bzip2 for delay signals

olding achieves 18.5 times. Soft thresholding shows a slight increase in the compression that is more visible in larger levels of decomposition. This happens because with soft thresholding, coefficients less than the chosen threshold are shrunk towards zero and the normalisation procedure has the side effect of zeroing coefficients relatively close to zero. Thus, the sequence of zeroes increases and RLE performs better in that case, rather than for the hard threshold method.

For the examined signals the hard thresholding technique performs better than the soft method regarding the reconstructed signal's quality. The compression ratio using soft thresholding is slightly greater, but choosing this method would increase the MSE to much higher values.

5.6   An examination of window sizes

This section examines the effect on compression ratio and reconstruction error of different window sizes applied on the measurements. As was mentioned before, the algorithm is applied on sequential data blocks. These blocks of data can be viewed as a window of collected measurements passed into the wavelet algorithm. An examination of the size of each of these blocks is presented here.

The experiment examines 30 signals of 4096 delay measurements. Each signal is split in multiple subfiles of 64 samples (see Fig. 5.22) and each subfile is analysed with wavelets at the maximum decomposition level (i.e. level 6) along with application of the GK threshold described in Section 5.3. The reconstruction files of the subfiles are concatenated together and the error is calculated from the total reconstruction against the original large file. The same procedure recurs for multiple subfiles of 128, 256, 1024, 2048,

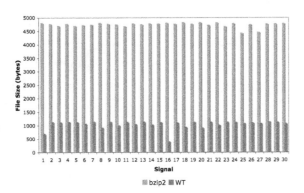

Figure 5.19: Compression performance of the wavelet algorithm (level 10 decomposition) against bzip2 for data rate signals

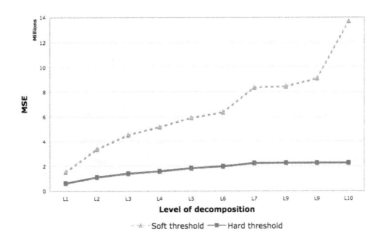

Figure 5.20: Average error of compression for hard and soft thresholds

4096 samples (in the case of 4096 samples there is only 1 file). The results for delay measurements are listed below in Figs. 5.23 and 5.24.

In general, it is intuitive to expect that with smaller windows, less compression and better quality of the reconstructed signal would be achieved. This happens because the algorithm adapts to smaller parts of the whole signal and analyses them individually. However, the bigger the window the greater the compression and the reconstruction error, as the algorithm has to adapt to larger parts of the total data. Thus, there is a trade off between compression and reconstruction quality.

In Fig. 5.24, however, there are some inconsistencies with the above general rule. Specifically, there are some cases (for example window size 512 and 256) where the bigger window offers more compression and less error. This, however, results from the examination of the thirty delay signals and is not a general conclusion. Figures 5.25, 5.26, 5.27 show the performance of error for all thirty signals. It can be seen that some signals perform better, both in terms of compression and quality, with window sizes relatively larger than others which, however, are not consistent for all signals. For example, series 10 in 5.25 performs better with a window size of 512 samples rather than a window size of 256. Series 7 in 5.27 performs better with a window size of 2048 samples rather than a window size of 512.

The optimal window size depends on the specific characteristics of the signal, its burstiness and the distribution of the burstiness, i.e. after windowing the signal some parts may include burstiness and some others not. In the case of signal 27 (series 7 in 5.27), when examined with a window size of 1024 it gives a smaller error in parts where the values are small (see Fig. 5.28) and bigger MSE where the values are large (see Fig. 5.30).

In contrast, when examining with a window size of 2048, there is a smaller

MSE for parts where the values are large (see Fig. 5.31) and a bigger MSE for parts where the values are small (see Fig. 5.29). So, in this case the error is smaller when examining this signal with a bigger window. However, this is an isolated case and most signals have greater error when analysed with bigger window as can be seen in Fig. 5.25, 5.26 and 5.27. There are 16 signals that give the best quality when examining with a window size of 64 samples and 3 signals that give best quality with a window size of 4096 samples.

Similar to the experiments above, the results in Figs. 5.32 and 5.33 show the results from 14 signals of 4096 data rate measurements. In this case the results follow the general rule of performance for compression and error reconstruction described previously.

5.7 Summary

In this chapter, Wavelet based denoising has been implemented in order to achieve lossy compression of network delay and data rate measurements while maintaining the characteristic features of the examined signals. Two techniques of coefficient threshold selection were studied and their behaviour on these types of signals was examined.

In general, the BM technique increases the MSE and C.R. as the level of decomposition increases. On the other hand, the GK method restricts C.R. for higher levels of decomposition whilst maintaining the quality of the reconstructed signals at reasonable levels.

For the delay signals, the BM technique gives better PSNR than the GK method only for the first two levels of decomposition. However, the offered C.R. for both of those levels is lower than the one offered by GK (see Tables

5.1, 5.3).

For data rate signals the BM technique does not give better average PSNR, than GK even at the first level. The same applies for the C.R. However, it gives more consistent PSNR values for data rate signals. For the BM method PSNR ranges from 49 dB to 52.8 dB at level 1 and 35.7 dB to 40.7 dB at level 2. By contrast, the GK method gives 39 dB to 58.6 dB and 37.2 dB to 58.1 dB (see Table 5.4).

The GK method is more appropriate for both types of signals as it offers more reasonable C.R. and good PSNR values even when reaching high levels of decomposition. It can adapt to bursty signals such as the case of signal 10 (Fig. 5.13) and it does not require any parameter, unlike the BM method. The reconstructed signals preserve quality for interesting features whilst smoothing out the detail information in non-significant parts of the signal. For delay signals level 6 seems to be more appropriate for decomposition as it offers the best balance between compression ratio and quality. Similarly, level 5 is more appropriate for data rate signals.

Because of the advantages of the Gupta Kaur algorithm over the Birge Massart (see Section 5.7) and the superiority of the hard threshold, these techniques were used further and the resulting compressing scores were compared with the results of the bzip2 compression tool.

On average, for delay signals the GK algorithm offered 6.5 times more compression than bzip2. For data rate signals, the achieved compression is 4.7 times more than bzip2.

Some improvements could be made in how the algorithm deals with the threshold in cases where spikes occur in an *already bursty signal* such as signal 16 (Fig. 5.17). This would lead to more control over the quality of the reconstructed signal and more consistent PSNR values. A possible solution would be the embedded zero-tree wavelet (EZW) transform proposed by [Sha93] as described in Chapter 7. The EZW algorithm can achieve high compression ratios by predicting insignificant wavelet coefficients across different scales while having a mechanism to control the PSNR of the reconstruction.

Finally, the effect of the window size (i.e. the length of the examined signal) is also discussed in this chapter. In general, the smaller the window size the less compression and better quality of the reconstructed signal. On the other hand, the bigger the window size, the greater the compression and the reconstruction error. However, there are some particular cases that a bigger window size offers more compression and less error.

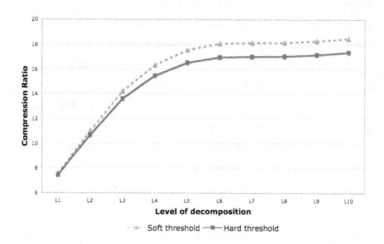

Figure 5.21: Performance of compression for hard and soft thresholds

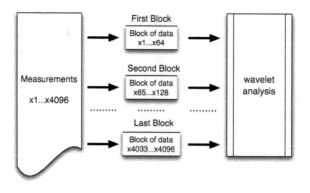

Figure 5.22: In this paragraph we are examining the size of each data block.

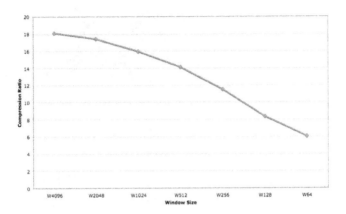

Figure 5.23: Average Compression Ratio for the 30 Delay signals with different window sizes

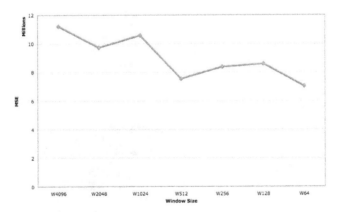

Figure 5.24: Average Mean Square Error for the 30 Delay signals with different window sizes

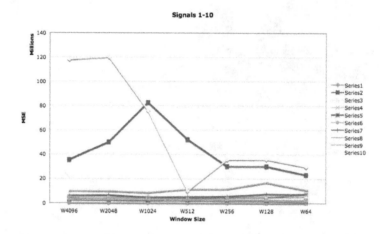

Figure 5.25: Mean Square Error for signals 1-10 (series 1 to 10)

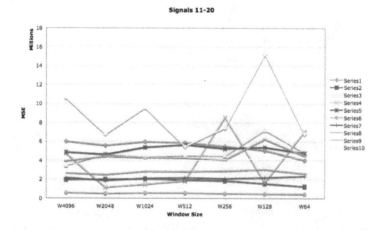

Figure 5.26: Mean Square Error for signals 11-20 (series 1 to 10)

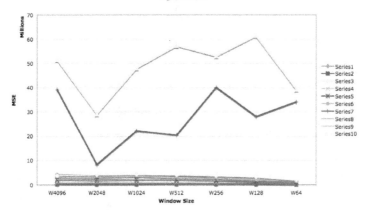

Figure 5.27: Mean Square Error for signals 21-30 (series 1 to 10)

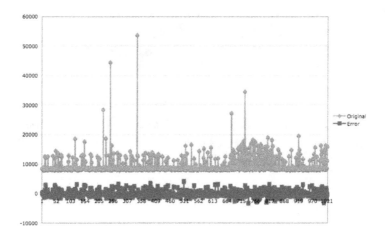

Figure 5.28: Samples 1...1024 of signal 27 examined with a window size of 1024. Note that error is less than in Fig. 5.29

100

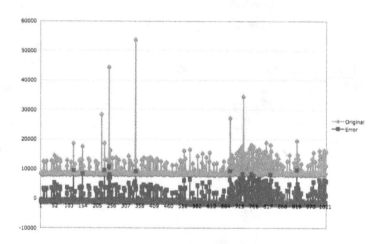

Figure 5.29: Samples 1...1024 of signal 27 examined with a window size of 2048

101

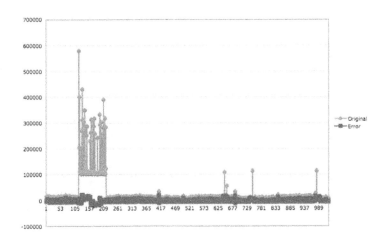

Figure 5.30: Samples 1025...2048 of signal 27 examined with a window size of 1024. Note that error is more than in Fig. 5.31

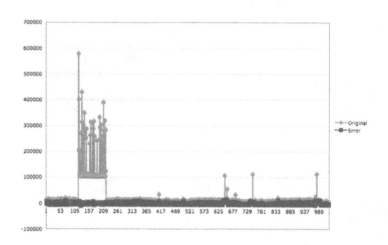

Figure 5.31: Samples 1025...2048 of signal 27 examined with a window size of 2048

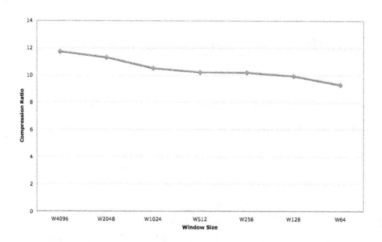

Figure 5.32: Average Compression Ratio for 14 Data Rate signals

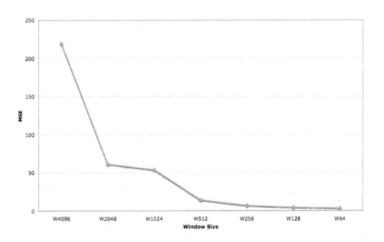

Figure 5.33: Average Mean Square Error for 14 Data Rate signals

CHAPTER 6

Analysing Performance

6.1 Introduction

This chapter is divided into five sections. In the first and second sections eight different wavelets are compared in terms of achievable compression ratio (Section 6.2) and their potential to preserve the energy of the reconstructed signal and its scaling behaviour (Section 6.3). The third section (6.4) describes the preservation of the quality of the reconstructed signal in terms of PSNR values and statistical metrics such as standard deviation and mean. The forth section (6.5) is focused on examining the preservation of the long range dependence characteristic. Finally, the fifth section (6.6) presents and discusses the results from the on-line implementation of the algorithm.

6.2 Wavelets and Compression Performance

The mother-wavelet chosen to analyse the network measurement signals is of prime importance as some wavelets offer better reconstruction quality and different compression ratios than others. However, there is no wavelet that gives the best results for all kinds of signals.

Eight wavelets were chosen and compared against each other in order to find out which one offers better reconstruction results after thresholding with the GK technique and hard threshold as described in Chapter 4. In all experiments the decomposition of the signals happened up to level 6 for both data rate and delay signals.

The following wavelets were compared: Haar, Meyer, Biorthogonal 3.9 and Daubechies D4, D6, D8, D10, D12. The index of Daubechies wavelets indicates the number of coefficients. The number of vanishing moments each Daubechies wavelet has is half of the number of coefficients, i.e. D4 has 2 vanishing moments.

Regarding speech and audio signals, [Agb96, NRIA03], among others, have found that for better reconstruction quality wavelets with many vanishing moments should be utilised, as they introduce less distortion and concentrate more signal energy in the approximation coefficients. Wavelets with many vanishing moments are described with many coefficients in the scaling and wavelet functions, thus increasing the computation overhead of the wavelet transform, the complexity of the algorithm and most importantly the output file size.

Tables 6.1 and 6.2 show the average compression ratio results for each of the above wavelets for the thirty delay and data rate signals described in Section 4.6. The Haar wavelet with the least vanishing moments gives the best results for delay signals and has the third place for data rate signals.

106

Even though Haar does not have the first place for data rate signals, it's compression ratio is very close to D4's that has the first place.

6.3 Wavelets and Signal Energy Preservation

6.3.1 Wavelet Energy Attributes

The first task of estimating the percentage of kept energy was split into two parts. The signals described in Section 4.6 were used as input and all eight wavelets were examined one by one. In the first part, the flow chart in Fig. 6.1 was followed in order to estimate the percentage of preserved energy in the approximation coefficients. The threshold was such that only the approximation coefficients were kept and all detail coefficients filtered out. The percentage of kept energy for each signal was calculated by the L^2-norm recovery criterion [MMOP04] given in percentage terms by:

$$PERFL2 = 100 * \left(\frac{l^2\text{-}norm(CXC)}{l^2\text{-}norm(C)} \right) \tag{6.1}$$

where CXC are the coefficients of the thresholded decomposition and C the coefficients of the original decomposition.

Tables 6.3 and 6.4 show the percentage of kept energy in the approximation coefficients at level 6 of decomposition for delay and data rate signals respectively.

For delay signals there is a significant difference in the percentage of preserved energy among the wavelets. For data rate signals the percentage of kept energy is very similar among wavelets. However, in both cases, the Haar wavelet has the worst score in preserving the energy.

Even though the reconstruction quality depends largely on the approximation coefficients, it also depends to some extent on the detail coefficients

107

Wavelet	Haar	D4	D6	D8	D10	D12	Meyer	Bio 3.9
Avg.	16.98	16.29	16.15	15.44	14.78	14.29	10.26	15.02
Min.	5.66	5.44	5.34	5.24	5.14	5.04	4.28	5.18
Max.	32.44	32.65	29.63	27.41	25.89	23.09	16.7	24.29
Rank	1	2	3	4	6	7	8	5

Table 6.1: Average Compression Ratio for 30 Delay Signals at Level 6 with various Wavelets

Wavelet	Haar	D4	D6	D8	D10	D12	Meyer	Bio 3.9
Avg.	11.20	11.23	11.33	10.84	10.53	10.34	8.45	10.47
Min.	10.32	10.08	9.87	9.66	9.44	9.23	7.68	9.30
Max.	27.43	33.44	33.54	34.48	32.56	31.37	21.88	33.44
Rank	3	2	1	4	5	7	8	6

Table 6.2: Average Compression Ratio for 30 Data Rate Signals at Level 6 with various Wavelets

Figure 6.1: Flow chart for Energy calculation in approximation coefficients.

Wavelet	Haar	D4	D6	D8	D10	D12	Meyer	Bio 3.9
Min. %	31.0	34.6	35.9	38.4	41.1	42.2	61.0	35.9
Max. %	95.7	97.2	97.6	97.6	97.7	97.8	98.6	95.3
Avg. %	63.34	69.68	71.58	73.59	74.61	76.08	86.22	73.38
Rank	8	7	6	4	3	2	1	5

Table 6.3: Percentage of Preserved Energy in Approximation Coefs. for Delay Signals at Level 6

Wavelet	Haar	D4	D6	D8	D10	D12	Meyer	Bio 3.9
Min. %	99.1	99.4	99.5	99.5	99.5	99.6	99.8	99.1
Max. %	99.8	99.9	99.9	99.9	99.9	99.9	100.0	99.9
Avg. %	99.73	99.82	99.84	99.86	99.87	99.88	99.93	99.79
Rank	8	6	5	4	3	2	1	7

Table 6.4: Percentage of Preserved Energy in Approximation Coefs. for Data Rate Signals at Level 6

preserved from the suggested thresholding algorithm.

In the second part of the energy preservation investigation, the flow chart in Fig. 6.2 was followed in order to estimate the percentage of preserved energy after applying the proposed threshold (GK and Hard threshold). In this case both approximation and detail coefficients are preserved. Again, the percentage of kept energy for each signal was calculated by equation (6.1).

Tables 6.5 and 6.6 show the percentage of kept energy in the coefficients after applying the proposed threshold at level 6 of decomposition for delay and data rate signals respectively.

Table 6.5 shows that the Haar wavelet ranks third in keeping the energy of delay signals after applying the proposed threshold. This is a significant improvement in comparison to the results of Table 6.3. For data rate signals (see Table 6.6) the inclusion of detail coefficients adds a very small percentage to the preserved energy as most of the energy is included in the approximation coefficients. In both cases, the average preserved energy is very high. It should be noted that including detail coefficients is essential for preserving the signal characteristics.

6.3.2 Wavelet Scaling Behaviour

In this section an energy plot (see 2.4.4) was generated for all 30 delay and data rate signals using all wavelets. This is done to examine how closely different wavelets preserve the scaling behaviour of the original signals.

The Haar wavelet gives the smallest error per scale in the energy plots. Fig. 6.3 and 6.5 show the common cases of scaling behaviour for data rate and delay signals respectively. In Fig. 6.4 and 6.6 are shown the worst case scenarios for data rate and delay signals respectively. The Haar wavelet gives the best results in most cases.

Figure 6.2: Flow chart for Energy calculation in thresholded coefficients

Wavelet	Haar	D4	D6	D8	D10	D12	Meyer	Bio 3.9
Min. %	97.06	96.88	96.57	95.95	96.70	96.22	96.60	96.91
Max. %	99.97	99.92	99.93	99.93	99.82	99.94	99.91	99.97
Avg. %	98.44	98.37	98.29	98.33	98.34	98.32	98.99	98.50
Rank	3	4	8	6	5	7	1	2

Table 6.5: Percentage of Preserved Energy in Thresholded Coefs. for Delay Signals at Level 6

Wavelet	Haar	D4	D6	D8	D10	D12	Meyer	Bio 3.9
Min. %	99.88	99.92	99.92	99.93	99.93	99.94	99.96	99.89
Max. %	100.00	100.00	100.00	100.00	100.00	100.00	100.00	100.00
Avg. %	99.99	99.99	99.99	100.00	99.99	100.00	100.00	99.99
Rank	2	2	2	1	2	1	1	2

Table 6.6: Percentage of Preserved Energy in Thresholded Coefs. for Data Rate Signals at Level 6

In order to quantify the findings, Tables 6.7 and 6.8 show the average relative percentage error of energy per scale for 30 delay and 30 data rate signals respectively. Similarly, Tables 6.9 and 6.10 show the maximum relative percentage error of energy per scale for delay and data rate signals respectively.

The reconstruction preserves very closely the scaling characteristics of both types of signals and even in the worst case scenarios, it offers better results than some advanced network traffic generation models. As a comparison, reference [VV06] provides a model with the aim of reproducing the scaling nature of real traffic. Even though the authors do not provide their error in the energy plots with numbers, it can be seen from the figures that the error in some cases is several dB, much more than in figures 6.4 and 6.6 where the error is less than half dB.

6.4   Wavelet Quality Attributes

For the second task of examining which wavelet offers best reconstruction results, two phases were followed; the decomposition and the reconstruction phases (see Fig. 4.1). In order to measure the quality of the reconstructed signals with different wavelets, the inverse wavelet transform was applied on the produced coefficients after thresholding.

The quality of the reconstruction signal was compared with the original by using the PSNR value as described in equations 2.1 and 2.2. Tables 6.11 and 6.12 show the average PSNR value after reconstruction at level 6 for the thirty delay and data rate signals respectively.

Tables 6.13 and 6.14 show the relative percentage error between the original and the reconstructed delay signals for the mean and standard deviation

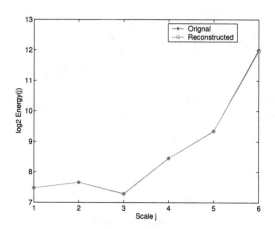

Figure 6.3: Energy scaling behaviour for data rate signal 22 with Haar analysis

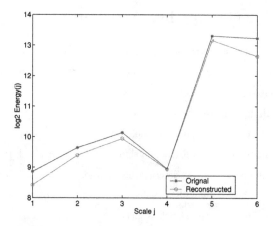

Figure 6.4: Energy scaling behaviour for data rate signal 16 with Haar analysis

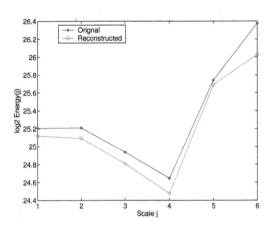

Figure 6.5: Energy scaling behaviour for delay signal 11 with Haar analysis

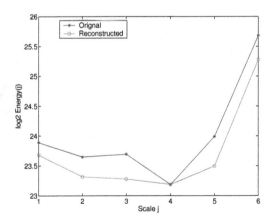

Figure 6.6: Energy scaling behaviour for delay signal 26 with Haar analysis

Wavelet	L1	L2	L3	L4	L5	L6
Haar	**3.860**	6.047	**7.355**	**7.573**	13.300	12.364
db4	5.241	6.848	9.883	12.588	13.231	12.793
db6	6.011	8.161	10.224	14.442	14.096	11.546
db8	6.011	7.790	10.004	14.609	15.570	11.821
db10	7.087	7.970	11.499	12.865	11.815	9.722
db12	7.040	8.289	11.005	15.303	14.037	11.175
dmey	6.557	6.704	12.609	13.549	12.768	**7.472**
bior3.9	7.070	**4.967**	9.056	12.179	**11.671**	7.763

Table 6.7: Average Relative Percentage Error of Energy Per Scale for 30 Delay Signals. Bold values indicate the minimum value per column

Wavelet	L1	L2	L3	L4	L5	L6
Haar	**1.024**	1.748	**1.024**	**0.592**	**1.046**	**2.219**
db4	2.202	**1.077**	1.356	1.563	6.572	5.141
db6	2.032	2.367	2.457	2.238	2.844	5.971
db8	1.474	2.701	1.977	1.062	4.053	9.932
db10	1.385	2.158	1.909	2.224	4.325	6.997
db12	1.162	1.693	2.021	3.064	3.254	6.013
dmey	1.135	1.167	1.784	1.809	1.164	4.187
bior3.9	1.485	2.225	1.492	2.174	5.297	8.500

Table 6.8: Average Relative Percentage Error of Energy Per Scale for 30 Data Rate Signals. Bold values indicate the minimum value per column

Wavelet	L1	L2	L3	L4	L5	L6
Haar	13.237	20.464	25.527	19.118	32.141	29.605
db4	17.106	21.244	35.92	38.551	36.39	36.568
db6	23.441	28.485	26.785	38.509	30.351	50.048
db8	17.782	25.303	23.399	32.191	39.972	35.382
db10	22.444	22.015	40.132	25.335	48.632	24.209
db12	21.893	24.624	29.246	40.855	38.065	72.783
dmey	18.116	19.31	29.514	40.753	32.831	25.562
bior3.9	26.152	16.402	33.709	35.16	24.171	43.971

Table 6.9: Maximum Relative Percentage Error of Energy Per Scale for 30 Delay Signals

Wavelet	L1	L2	L3	L4	L5	L6
Haar	26.119	32.876	13.17	8.698	10.955	33.504
db4	31.426	25.306	17.969	15.467	76.53	26.841
db6	30.247	35.009	27.858	27.14	36.806	27.685
db8	40.213	29.855	22.764	20.212	23.591	31.878
db10	38.51	36.107	38.414	15.096	30.939	30.244
db12	30.992	25.764	29.777	35.073	26.984	31.288
dmey	30.629	30.542	33.385	21.294	13.233	27.915
bior3.9	39.618	34.448	26.301	25.771	57.631	36.043

Table 6.10: Maximum Relative Percentage Error of Energy Per Scale for 30 Data Rate Signals

respectively. Similarly, Tables 6.15 and 6.16 for the data rate signals.

As can be inferred from the tables, wavelets with more vanishing moments do not provide higher PSNR values for the reconstructed signals. Even though the Haar wavelet misses some detail and does not always represent detail at all resolution scales, it ranks first on average in both delay and data rate signals in terms of quality of results.

Specifically, for delay signals, the Haar wavelet gives the best PSNR for all signals and for data rate signals, it is the best option on average. The better performance of the Haar wavelet can be explained if we consider the fact that the value of the produced coefficients simply indicates how similar the selected wavelet is to the corresponding part of the examined signal [MMOP04]. The closer the similarity the greater the value of the coefficient. Wavelets have different characteristics and their forms can be seen in Fig. 6.7.

For most cases, the wavelets are not as similar to the examined signals as is the Haar wavelet. For this reason, the produced coefficients have smaller values which means that more coefficients are thresholded during the compression process. This does not happen as frequently when using the Haar wavelet. As a result, the reconstruction quality in those cases is better when using the Haar wavelet.

Wavelet	Haar	D4	D6	D8	D10	D12	Meyer	Bio 3.9
Min. PSNR	32.8	32.1	31.6	31.5	31.3	31.7	31.0	31.4
Max. PSNR	50.1	46.8	45.4	45.5	45.2	44.8	46.0	45.8
Avg. PSNR	39.6	38.2	37.6	37.5	37	37	37.1	37.3
Rank	1	2	3	4	7	8	6	5

Table 6.11: PSNR Values for Delay Signals After Reconstruction

Wavelet	Haar	D4	D6	D8	D10	D12	Meyer	Bio 3.9
Min. PSNR	34.0	34.4	34.2	34.2	33.6	34.0	34.5	34.0
Max. PSNR	57.2	59.9	59.0	59.1	58.0	58.7	57.9	60.4
Avg. PSNR	53.4	51.6	51.7	49.7	50.8	51.5	53.0	50.4
Rank	1	3	4	8	6	5	2	7

Table 6.12: PSNR Values for Data Rate Signals After Reconstruction

Wavelet	Haar	D4	D6	D8	D10	D12	Meyer	Bio 3.9
Min. Error	0.00	0.01	0.00	0.00	0.00	0.00	0.00	0.01
Max. Error	0.21	0.28	0.50	1.57	1.04	2.39	0.67	0.36
Avg. Error	0.03	0.08	0.11	0.16	0.15	0.15	0.10	0.11

Table 6.13: Relative Percentage Error of Mean Values for Delay Signals After Reconstruction

Wavelet	Haar	D4	D6	D8	D10	D12	Meyer	Bio 3.9
Min. Error	0.03	0.05	0.11	0.14	0.18	0.16	0.04	0.01
Max. Error	7.26	8.62	10.50	9.34	10.03	11.29	11.41	5.62
Avg. Error	2.57	3.23	3.72	3.82	4.00	4.24	3.60	1.50

Table 6.14: Relative Percentage Error of Standard Deviation Values for Delay Signals After Reconstruction

Wavelet	Haar	D4	D6	D8	D10	D12	Meyer	Bio 3.9
Min. Error	0.00	0.00	0.00	0.00	0.00	0.00	0.00	0.00
Max. Error	0.12	0.14	0.10	0.11	0.11	0.09	0.10	0.15
Avg. Error	0.02	0.03	0.03	0.03	0.04	0.04	0.03	0.04

Table 6.15: Relative Percentage Error of Mean Values for Data Rate Signals After Reconstruction

Wavelet	Haar	D4	D6	D8	D10	D12	Meyer	Bio 3.9
Min. Error	0.01	0.00	0.00	0.01	0.00	0.02	0.09	0.00
Max. Error	0.88	0.79	1.07	1.06	1.35	1.04	0.94	0.53
Avg. Error	0.16	0.20	0.17	0.18	0.18	0.18	0.34	0.16

Table 6.16: Relative Percentage Error of Standard Deviation Values for Data Rate Signals After Reconstruction

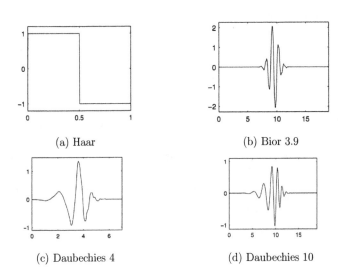

(a) Haar

(b) Bior 3.9

(c) Daubechies 4

(d) Daubechies 10

Figure 6.7: Examples of different wavelet forms.

The Haar wavelet is the simplest wavelet algorithm that can give perfect reconstruction (when no coefficients are removed) and has the following additional advantages [Nie99] [Kapb]:

- It is conceptually simple

- Fast

- Memory efficient

- Offers higher compression than other wavelets

- and is exactly reversible without producing edge effects.

6.5 Self Similarity, Long Range Dependence and the Hurst Parameter

Leland et al., with their well-known publication in 1994 [LTWW94], showed that Ethernet LAN traffic does not follow the Poisson model as was commonly assumed. They proved that Ethernet LAN traffic is self-similar i.e. that network traffic is bursty across a wide range of time scales.

Self-similarity can be described as the property of a data set to look or behave the same when viewed at different time or space scales [AKR]. Some self-similar processes are given in [Ros96]. Self-similarity of network traffic depends on the network utilisation level and can be described by the Hurst parameter [LTWW94].

The long-range dependence (LRD) is one of the properties that self-similar processes have and it can also be described by the Hurst parameter [Ros96]. It is a way to measure the memory of a process or, in other words, how correlated distant events of a process are. By examining the autocorrelation function (ACF) of a LRD process we can find out how similar that process is with shifted versions of itself [AKR]. For LRD data, the ACF follows a power-law behaviour (i.e. slowly decaying) whereas for short-range dependence data the ACF decays exponentially (i.e. quickly decaying) [AKR].

In recent years, many studies have been conducted observing the self-similarity and long-range dependence phenomena in various networking contexts like ATM, VBR video and the world-wide-web (WWW) [CB97, WPRT01, RW00, ST99, FGWK98, VKMV00]. Furthermore, many studies have concluded that LRD significantly increases queuing delays and leads to packet loss [PF95, HFW01]. The above issues have led the network community to become involved in identifying and measuring the Hurst parameter in order to perform a better signal analysis.

There is no definite way yet found to precisely calculate the Hurst parameter. In addition, there are various Hurst value estimators and each one has its own shortcomings and merits. A comparison of various Hurst estimators is presented in [KFR02].

In general, the higher the value of the Hurst parameter H the longer the LRD. For a random signal $H = 0.5$ this means that there is no LRD in the signal. If H is greater than 0.5, then this indicates a persistent behaviour (large values followed by large values and small values followed by small) whereas if H is less than 0.5, it indicates a non-persistent behaviour also known as a reverting process or "mean reversion" (an increase will tend to be followed by a decrease and vice-verca) [Naw95].

6.5.1 The Rescaled Adjusted Range Statistic

For the estimation of the Hurst parameter an algorithm was developed based on the rescaled range (R/S) statistic. The R/S statistic is the range of partial sums of deviations of a time series from its mean, rescaled by its standard deviation [Naw95].

For a given set of n samples $(X_1, X_2, X_3, ..., X_n)$, with sample mean $\bar{X}(n)$ and sample standard deviation $S(n)$, the classic rescaled adjusted range statistic for that particular set of samples is given by the following equation [LTWW94]

$$\frac{R(n)}{S(n)} = \frac{1}{S(n)} \left[max(0, W_1, W_2, ..., W_n) - min(0, W_1, W_2, ..., W_n) \right] \quad (6.2)$$

where

$$W_k = (X_1 + X_2 + ... + X_k) - k\bar{X}(n) \quad (6.3)$$

and $k = 1, 2, 3, 4, ..., n$

By combining 6.2 and 6.3 we can get the following equation [Naw95]:

$$\frac{R(n)}{S(n)} = \frac{1}{S(n)} \left[max_{1<k<n} \left(\sum_{j=1}^{k} [X_j - \bar{X}(n)] \right) - min_{1<k<n} \left(\sum_{j=1}^{k} [X_j - \bar{X}(n)] \right) \right]$$
$$(6.4)$$

Hurst observed that the following equation well represents the relation between the R/S statistic expectation and the Hurst parameter [LTWW94]:

$$E\left[\frac{R(n)}{S(n)} \right] = an^H \quad as \quad n \to \infty \quad (6.5)$$

where a is a constant. By taking the log transformation of 6.5 we have:

$$log\left(E\left[\frac{R(n)}{S(n)} \right] \right) = log(a) + Hlog(n) \quad (6.6)$$

The final step involves plotting the log of $R(n)/S(n)$ versus the log of the sample region $[1, n]$. This process produces the R/S plot also called a pox diagram.

By performing regression analysis, a least squares line is fitted to the points of the R/S plot. However, the edge values of the sample region are not considered. This is because for the smallest samples, the R/S values are biased due to short-range correlations; whereas for the largest samples the R/S values are statistically insignificant [Ros96, Naw95]. The slope of the regression line is an estimate of the Hurst parameter [LTWW94, Naw95].

6.5.2 Goodness of fit calculation

In order to estimate the error of the drawn regression line, the goodness of fit of the linear regression was calculated. The "goodness of fit", denoted by r^2, has no units and is given by the following expression [DS04]:

$$r^2 = 1 - \frac{SS_{reg}}{SS_{tot}} \tag{6.7}$$

where

$$SS_{reg} = \sum_{i=1}^{n}(y_i - y_i')^2 \tag{6.8}$$

$$SS_{tot} = \sum_{i=1}^{n}(y_i - \bar{y}_i)^2 \tag{6.9}$$

The variable i represents a sample and takes values between 1 and n, where n is the total number of samples.

- y_i is the actual log R/S value of sample i

- y_i' is the regression line estimate value for sample i

- $\bar{y}$ is the mean of log values of R/S statistic for the total range of samples

6.5.3 The Rescaled Range Statistic Block Algorithm

A variation of the classic R/S statistic was used as a Hurst estimation algorithm (Figure 6.8). This involved dividing the whole data set of n samples into $\lfloor n/N \rfloor$ non-overlapping sample blocks; where $1 \leq N \leq n$ is the sample block size. The calculations for the rescaled range value presented in Section 6.5.1 apply recursively to each sample block and ultimately produce $\lfloor n/N \rfloor$ intermediate R/S values. These intermediate values are cumulated and divided by the number of sample blocks in order to find the average R/S value for the current sample block size. The whole process repeats for all values that the sample block size can take $(1 \leq N \leq n)$ [LTWW94].

The above R/S statistic variation uses non-overlapping blocks of samples. However, there are other variations that use overlapping blocks or are limited to data sizes that are a power of two [Kapa].

As was mentioned in Section 6.5.1, for the regression analysis the edge values should not be considered. Thus, in order to exclude the edge values, a window that includes 90% of the data trace values was utilised. The window slides through the data trace and for each position of the window a regression line is calculated.

The Hurst parameter is estimated based on the gradient of the regression line with the best goodness of fit value. The R/S algorithm flowchart is presented below:

6.5.4 Long Range Dependence Preservation

The Hurst parameters of the original and reconstructed data rate signals were estimated following the algorithm described in the previous section and

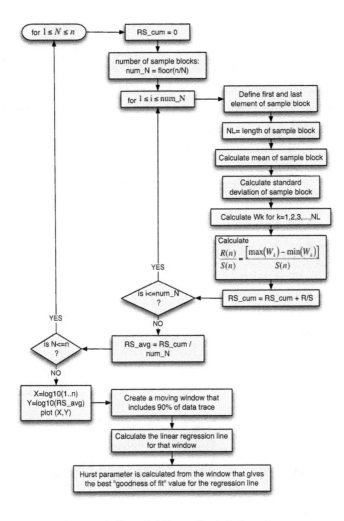

Figure 6.8: Rescaled Range Statistic flow chart

presented in Figure 6.8. Only data rate signals were examined as data rate expresses a traffic arrival process and long range dependence is usually examined in arrival processes.

Figure 6.9 shows the Hurst values for all thirty signals before and after the compression. It should be noted that the values presented in the graph are greater than the maximum value Hurst may have which is 1. However, the focus of this experiment was not to accurately estimate the Hurst value but to examine the error in the Hurst value before and after the compression.

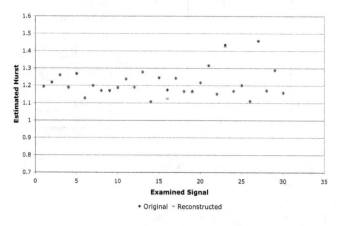

Figure 6.9: Hurst values for 30 original and compressed data rate signals

Table 6.17 shows the relative percentage error of the reconstructed Hurst values for all 30 data rate signals. From table 6.17 it can be seen that the maximum error is less than 5% (4.185%) and on average the error is 0.146% which occurs when examining signal 16.

Signal	Percentage Relative Error
Signal 1	-0.192
Signal 2	0.353
Signal 3	0.087
Signal 4	-0.252
Signal 5	0.355
Signal 6	-0.177
Signal 7	0.017
Signal 8	0.077
Signal 9	0.222
Signal 10	-0.025
Signal 11	-0.081
Signal 12	-0.076
Signal 13	-0.047
Signal 14	0.108
Signal 15	0.177
Signal 16	**-4.185**
Signal 17	-0.008
Signal 18	-0.111
Signal 19	-0.368
Signal 20	-0.025
Signal 21	0.122
Signal 22	0.017
Signal 23	-0.592
Signal 24	-0.017
Signal 25	-0.108
Signal 26	-0.009
Signal 27	0.26
Signal 28	-0.017
Signal 29	0.085
Signal 30	0.043

Table 6.17: Relative Percentage Error of Hurst Values for Data Rate Signals After Reconstruction

6.6 On-line Experiments

6.6.1 Practical Implementation

The full GK algorithm has been implemented by the author as a module for CoMo [IDM+04]. CoMo is a passive monitoring platform developed for the purpose of monitoring network links at high speeds and replying to real-time queries regarding network statistics.

CoMo has various modules that calculate one or more network measurements. There are some built-in modules that come with CoMo but it can also accept third-party modules. The proposed GK algorithm can be imbedded in the modules and compress the calculated measurements. When CoMo receives a query, the information is first decompressed and then shown to the end user.

CoMo's first aim is to capture the packets that arrive at the monitoring node. Then, the module-dependent statistics of the packets (for example packet length) are binned per second (or at any other specified time interval) thus producing measurements per second (for example data rate).

In order to examine the wavelet compression scheme in practical operation, two CoMo modules are written by the author and compared against each other. Compression is implemented only in one module. Both modules count bytes per second (data rate) and store a timestamp for each captured block of 1024 samples. Timestamps are required and help in replying to queries about statistics for a particular time period.

More specifically, packet information is aggregated per second and the resulting value represents one element of the 1024 signal samples. Thus, each block of samples spans a duration of 1024 seconds i.e. 17.06 minutes. However, only one module performs compression and passes the block of samples through the compression algorithm while the next block of 1024 samples is being captured and calculated.

As each data rate sample is generated in 1 second (an aggregated measurement per second), the analysis and compression processes are actually *independent of the bandwidth* of the link being monitored. There is a window of around 17 minutes for the analysis and compression phases to complete before the next block of 1024 measurements takes its turn. So, calculation time of the algorithm is not really an issue for this specific on-line implementation of the compression algorithm, as a few milliseconds of processing time are adequate for each block of measurements.

For the same reasons, the described system is scalable to high data rates as long as the measurements are aggregated. So, no matter what the bandwidth of the monitored link is, there will always be 1024 samples in each data block and each block will always span 17.06 minutes. The compression and quality results of the reconstructed signal only depend on the original signal characteristics and attributes (for example if it is bursty or not) and not on the bandwidth of the monitored link.

The window size of 1024 was chosen as it is a power of two and wavelet algorithms are more efficient and simple to implement with signal lengths of powers of two. There is no ideal window size for all situations as the window size is dependent on the characteristics and the type of each examined signal. However, as a general rule, the bigger the window-size the more the compression and the greater the reconstructed error. An examination of the performance of different window sizes is presented in Section 5.6.

6.6.2   Practical Results

The experiment lasted for 8 days and CoMo was monitoring traffic recorded on a research group's live network. This network supported up to 20 users using a mixture of machines running Windows, Linux and Mac OS X operating systems. Activities ranged from standard office and email applications to real time media and games sessions associated with research activities and dedicated research related operations including remote log retrieval. The overall traffic mix would be expected to show considerable variation.

The overall achieved compression for the whole signal is 34.5 times. The wavelet analysis, thresholding and compression takes place up to level 6 of decomposition. Fig. 6.10 presents a segment of 34 minutes from the 8 day duration experiment. This signal is characterised by discrete bursts of data rate. Some bursts have an amplitude of 70 kB/s while others are half that size or less. The reconstruction keeps intact the peaks and smoothes out the relatively small variation of the signal. PSNR for that segment is 55.9 dB.

The 34 minute signal is actually analysed as two blocks of 1024 samples, i.e. two blocks of 17 minute duration. Thus, it's statistics and energy scaling behaviour are presented in two different tables and two different figures. Table 6.18 shows the statistics for the first part and Table 6.19 for the second part. Respectively Fig. 6.11 shows the energy scaling behaviour for the first part and Fig. 6.12 for the second.

For the 34 minute signal, as can be inferred from the tables, the relative errors for mean, standard deviation and energy are very small. Fig. 6.11 shows a maximum energy divergence of 0.2 dB at scale 5 of decomposition. In the graph the difference looks significant but this is due the small scale in this particular figure. Fig. 6.12 shows a maximum energy divergence of 0.12 dB at scale 5 of decomposition. For all other scales, for both Fig. 6.11 and

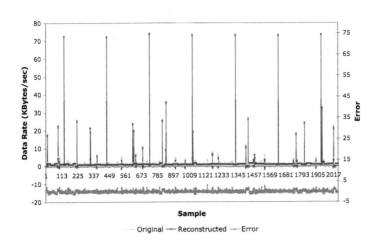

Figure 6.10: Data rate signal of 34 minutes compressed live by CoMo. Error is given on the secondary y-axis on the right (lower line). PSNR = 55.9 dB.

132

6.12 the energy of the reconstructed signal is almost identical to the energy of the original signal.

Statistic	Original	Reconstructed	Percentage Error
Mean	1364.51	1365.52	0.074%
Standard deviation	4511.83	4482.70	-0.64%
Energy	22218574	21959308	-1.16%

Table 6.18: Percentage Relative Error of Three Statistics for the First Part of 34 Minute Signal

Statistic	Original	Reconstructed	Percentage Error
Mean	1392.78	1392.86	0.005%
Standard deviation	4913.17	4879.3	-0.689%
Energy	26079122.39	25747639	-1.27%

Table 6.19: Percentage Relative Error of Three Statistics for the Second Part of 34 Minute Signal

Another segment of duration 17 minutes is presented in Fig. 6.13. The two high peaks at the beginning and end of the signal are preserved and the small variation from sample 150 up to 400 is smoothed. The medium amplitude peaks in the region of sample 400 up to 950 are also preserved but with more distortion in comparison to the highest peaks. PSNR for this signal is 34.4 dB.

Table 6.20 shows the percentage relative error for mean, standard deviation and the energy between the reconstructed and the original signal. The first two order statistics are preserved with very high accuracy. Fig. 6.14 shows the energy scaling behaviour of the original and reconstructed signals. The behaviour is almost identical.

6.7 Summary

In this chapter, eight wavelets have been compared for three different characteristics: energy preservation, scaling behaviour preservation and quality of reconstruction. Due to the fact that each wavelet has its own characteristics and different wavelets approximate parts of the analysed signal with different degree of accuracy, the results vary with each wavelet. The Haar wavelet, however, shows a consistency in describing better the analysed signals and has the best performance on average. Other advantages of the Haar wavelet are its conceptually simplicity, its fastness and memory efficiency and that it does not produce artefacts in the reconstructed signal.

Self-similarity of network traffic depends on the network utilisation level and is described by the Hurst parameter. The long-range dependence (LRD) is one of the properties that self-similar processes have and it can also be described by the Hurst parameter. For LRD data, the ACF follows a power-

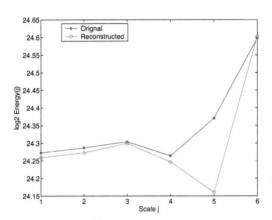

Figure 6.11: Energy behaviour across scales for first half of 34 minute on-line signal.

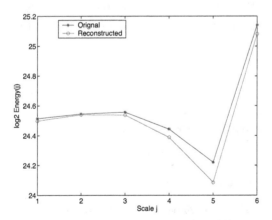

Figure 6.12: Energy behaviour across scales for second half of 34 minute on-line signal.

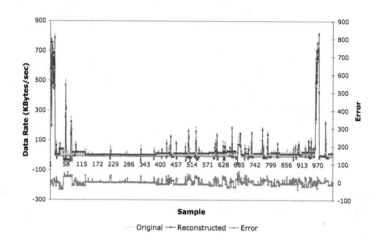

Figure 6.13: Data rate signal of 17 minutes compressed live by CoMo. Error is given on the secondary y-axis on the right (lower line). PSNR = 34.4 dB.

Statistic	Original	Reconstructed	Percentage Error
Mean	30712.799	30556.62	-0.5%
Standard deviation	107992.10	106930.84	-0.98%
Energy	12605569898	12367912005	-1.88%

Table 6.20: Percentage Relative Error of Three Statistics for 17 Minute Signal

law behaviour (i.e. slowly decaying) whereas for short-range dependence data the ACF decays exponentially (i.e. quickly decaying). In recent years, many studies have been conducted observing the self-similarity and long-range dependence phenomena in various networking contexts.

In this chapter the rescaled adjusted range statistic algorithm has been described, which is used for the estimation of the Hurst parameter. The Hurst value itself is of no direct concern in this research. However, the error in the Hurst parameter after analysing and compressing each signal is of concern as this value should be preserved. The experiments run on data rate signals have a maximum relative percentage error of 4.185 %

Finally, this chapter presents the results in terms of compression ratio, quality, spike preservation, statistics and energy scaling behaviour of data rate measurements from a real network. The overall achieved compression for the whole signal was 34.5 times. The analysis and compression were done on line in a research office facility that supported up to 20 researchers using a variety of network applications. It should be noted that because the measurements from the monitoring link are binned in a pre-specifed time interval, there are no issues with the processing time and the compression ratios are totally independent from the bandwidth of the link.

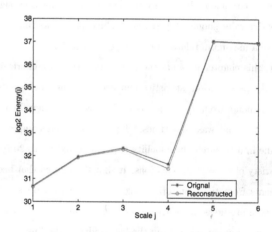

Figure 6.14: Energy behaviour across scales for 17 minute on-line signal.

CHAPTER 7

PSNR Controlled Compression

7.1 Introduction

The Gupta-Kaur threshold selection discussed in Chapter 5 calculated statistics from the absolute value of the coefficients and used these to select a threshold. However, in some cases, some significant coefficients were "hidden" by their statistical insignificance and thus were discarded. This had a negative effect on the level of quality in the reconstructed form of some signals. An extension to this work would therefore be a method of controlling the quality of the decompressed signal.

In this chapter Shapiro's proposed Embedded Zero-tree Wavelet (EZW) algorithm [Sha93] is used in order to develop a method for compressing various computer network measurements while having control over the reconstructed signals quality. The algorithm should maintain the characteristic and interesting features of the signal as described in Section 2.4.4.

Embedded encoding or progressive encoding is a method of compressing with increasing accuracy, i.e. the bits are generated in order of importance. For a specific bit rate encoding, all encodings of the same signal at lower bit rates are included in the beginning of the bit stream.

The algorithm was applied to the same network delay and data rate signals as described before. Experimental results were obtained to examine how the applied method behaves in terms of C.R. and a comparison is given against results from the lossless compression tool bzip2. The quality of reconstructed signals is measured by using the PSNR.

The rest of the chapter is structured as follows. In Section 7.2 the advantages of EZW are presented and the hypothesis and theory behind the algorithm is discussed. The algorithm itself is also explained along with some discussion regarding the advantages of arithmetic coding. In Section 7.3 the methodology followed for producing the simulation results is presented and the results are given in Section 7.4. Finally, conclusions and ideas for future work are given in Section 7.6.

7.2 EZW algorithm

In this section the characteristic features of EZW are presented along with its advantages. A deeper explanation of the actual encoding process follows. For encoding the outputs of the EZW algorithm, an arithmetic coder is utilised and the preference over the more commonly used Huffman coding is also explained in this section.

The EZW algorithm is based on the following key features [Sha93, MLA97]:

- The Discrete Wavelet Transform (DWT) is used to provide a multi-

141

resolution representation of the examined signal.

- The Successive Approximation notion, as its name implies, offers successively smaller uncertainty intervals regarding the value of a significant coefficient.

- During the dominant pass at the decoder side, the same zero-trees as in the encoder side are generated, thus recreating the same significance map with the encoder.

- During the sub-ordinate pass at the decoder side the mid-point of the uncertainty interval (defined by the current threshold) is assigned to the significant coefficient.

- The adaptive (multilevel) arithmetic coding is an entropy coder that requires nor training neither a pre-stored code table. It is used to encode the output from the dominant and sub-ordinate passes.

7.2.1 Advantages of EZW

By exploiting the self-similarity across different scales of the wavelet analysed signal, the EZW algorithm can achieve high compression ratios without requiring any knowledge of the source signal, prior training or pre-stored coding tables. The significance map of the coefficients, i.e. the coordinates of significant coefficients, is efficiently coded using a zero tree algorithm, described later in Section 7.2.2.

Because of the progressive nature of the algorithm, EZW offers the ability to stop the encoder when a specified target bit rate has been reached or when the reconstructed quality has reached the desirable levels.

Another attribute of EZW is that it compares each individual coefficient with a specific set of thresholds in order to determine significance. In contrast with other techniques, no statistics for sub-bands of wavelet coefficients are calculated. As a result, significant fine scale coefficients are not hidden because of their statistical insignificance.

7.2.2 The Zero-Tree structure

After the multi-scale analysis performed by the DWT, the signal is transformed to the wavelet domain where each coefficient in a given scale is related to a set of coefficients in a finer scale.

A coefficient at a coarse scale is named a "parent" and all coefficients at the next finer scale describing the same spatial or time location are its "children". These "children" similarly may have other "children" coefficients that are referred as "descendants" of the "parent" coefficient. For a given coefficient, all coefficients at all coarser scales are called "ancestors" of that coefficient.

The hypothesis in the EZW algorithm is that if a coefficient x at a given scale is insignificant with respect to the current threshold (i.e. $|x| < T$), then all its descendants are likely to be insignificant too.

For a given threshold T, a coefficient is an element of the zero-tree if itself and all its descendants are insignificant with respect to that threshold. If that element has no insignificant ancestors then it is the root of the zero-tree.

If a coefficient is insignificant with respect to a threshold T but one or more of its descendants is significant then that coefficient is described as an "isolated zero".

7.2.3 Encoding The Significance Map

In order to efficiently encode the position of significant coefficients each individual coefficient is compared against a set of thresholds. The initial threshold is chosen so that it fulfils the following equation:

$$\frac{C_{max}}{2} < T_0 \leq C_{max} \tag{7.1}$$

where C_{max} is the maximum value of coefficients and T_0 the initial threshold.

The wavelet coefficients so generated are scanned in such an order that no children coefficients are scanned before their parents. Also coarser levels are scanned before the finer ones. Fig. 7.1 shows the order in which coefficients are scanned for a 16-point signal. It should be noted that there should be 2 approximation coefficients left after the analysis. Therefore, the wavelet analysis should be applied up to the penultimate level of decomposition. Thus, for a 16-point signal the final level of decomposition should be level 3 (see Fig. 3.7) [MLA97].

When a coefficient is scanned, it is sent through Shapiro's flow chart of significance map encoding (see Fig. 7.2) [Sha93]. There are four possible outcomes and each outcome is assigned a symbol:

1. The coefficient is larger than T_0 and is positive (P)

2. The coefficient is larger than T_0 and is negative (N)

3. The coefficient is a zero-tree root (ZT) or

4. an isolated zero (IZ). There is no symbol generated for an element belonging in the zero-tree except for the root.

144

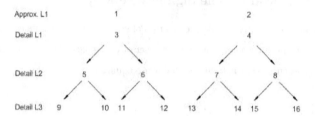

Figure 7.1: Scan order for 1-D EZW algorithm. Numbers represent the order that coefficients should be scanned.

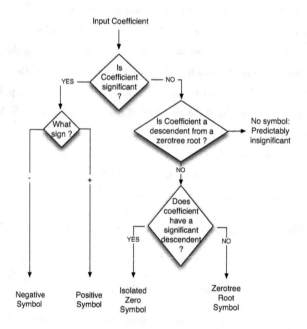

Figure 7.2: Flow chart for encoding a coefficient of the significance map

7.2.4 Dominant and Sub-ordinate Passes

During the encoding and decoding phases of EZW, two lists are scanned once. The dominant list contains coordinates of coefficients not found to be significant for the current threshold. The sub-ordinate list contains refinements of the significant coefficients and provides the successive approximation feature of EZW.

The EZW algorithm is mainly divided into 2 passes, the dominant and sub-ordinate passes. The dominant pass uses the dominant list to encode the significance map (as described in the previous section) and creates the sub-ordinate list, which contains values of significant coefficients. The encoded string of symbols (P, N, ZT, IZ) that describes the significant map is then entropy encoded using the adaptive arithmetic coder.

When a coefficient is found to be significant, it is replaced by a 0 in the dominant list, so that it does not prevent the occurrence of a zero-tree in later scans. When a zero-tree coefficient is found, all of its descendants are booked as insignificant and are not compared with the current threshold.

The sub-ordinate list is used in the sub-ordinate pass to decrease the uncertainty interval of a significant coefficient. For a given threshold T, a significant coefficient c belongs in the interval of $T < c < 2 * T$. The subordinate pass generates a 1 if the coefficient is in the upper half of the interval or a 0 if it belongs on the lower half (Fig. 7.3). Afterwards, the sequence of zeros and ones is entropy encoded with an adaptive arithmetic coder.

In the original algorithm proposal by Shapiro, after the sub-ordinate pass, the magnitudes in the sub-ordinate list are ordered in decreasing magnitude. However, in our implementation this sorting does not take place since the gain seems to be very small and the computational costs very high [ARRE95].

146

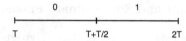

Figure 7.3: Subordinate pass uncertainty intervals. T represents a threshold.
Each coefficient is compared against T+ T/2 and a 0 or a 1 is produced
accordingly.

After the end of the sub-ordinate pass, the threshold is halved and the
next dominant pass takes place and so on. Only the coefficients not found to
be significant are scanned. The encoder then needs to send the dominant and
sub-ordinate pass outputs along with the initial threshold to the decoder.

7.2.5   Arithmetic coding

Arithmetic coding is a statistical entropy encoding method for lossless data
compression. It is very similar to Huffman coding as it assigns many bits to
low probability symbols and fewer bits to high probability symbols. The main
difference is that instead of replacing every individual symbol in the input
message with a code word, arithmetic coding encodes the whole message
with a fraction number in the region of $[0.0 \leq n < 1.0]$. For that reason,
arithmetic coding can approach optimal entropy encoding more closely than
Huffman encoding [HV91].

There are two models for arithmetic coding, the static and the adaptive
model. The static model has a predetermined knowledge of symbol probabilities, usually obtained by scanning the input message and calculating
the probabilities. The adaptive model assumes a uniform distribution and
adjusts the probabilities of each symbol, as the input message is encoded/de-
coded [HV91].

7.3 Methodology

For the purpose of examining the behaviour of the EZW technique, 30 delay and 30 data rate measurement signals (described in Section 4.6) were used as inputs to the algorithm. Each signal had 1024 measurement points and was decomposed up to level 9 for the reason explained in Section 7.2.3, using the Haar wavelet. The Haar wavelet was chosen because of the reasons described in Chapter 6.

The methodology flow chart is presented in Fig. 7.4. After the wavelet decomposition, the EZW encoder attempts to encode the wavelet coefficients by sequentially dividing the threshold by two. In each run, after decoding the symbols, the inverse wavelet transform is applied and the PSNR of the reconstructed signal is calculated to estimate the reconstruction quality.

If the PSNR value is not higher than a predetermined desired value (x in Fig. 7.4), then the EZW encoder continues to halve the threshold and encodes more detail coefficients. Otherwise, the outputs from the dominant and subordinate passes are passed through the arithmetic encoder.

To reconstruct the signal, the stored arithmetic coded output is passed through the arithmetic decoder, the EZW decoder and lastly through the inverse wavelet algorithm.

The individual C.R. results are calculated from the ratio of the original file size over the sum of file sizes of the encoded dominant and sub-ordinate file sizes.

The following PSNR and C.R. values in Section 7.4 refer to the average over these 30 signals (delay or data rate) except when explicitly noting for which signal they refer.

In addition to the quantitative measurement of the reconstruction quality, figures are also included in order to present the original signal, the re-

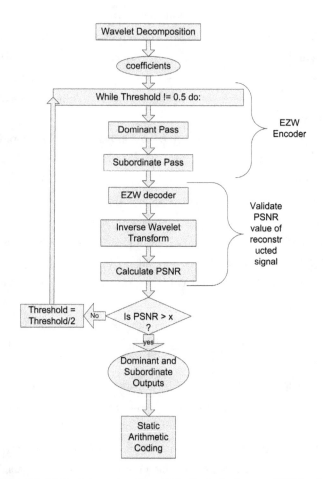

Figure 7.4: Methodology algorithm. X is the desired target PSNR value

constructed signal after compression and the error between them.

7.4 EZW Algorithm Results

Table 7.1 and Table 7.2 show the average PSNR and average C.R. results over 30 experiments for delay and data rate signals respectively. The target PSNR is set to 36 dB, 38 dB, 40 dB, 42 dB and 44 dB for both cases.

As expected the higher the target PSNR is, the lower the achievable C.R. Data rate signals are compressed less than delay signals because they include more fluctuation, which amounts to high frequency components that need to be preserved in order for the quality to reach the required amount.

As explained in Section 7.2, by lowering the threshold more detail is encoded by the EZW algorithm in order to increase the quality of the reconstructed signal and reach a specified target PSNR value. That value, however, indicates a lower limit that the quality should have and the average PSNR is usually higher than that. This happens because by lowering the threshold, the PSNR may increase by fractions of dB or even up to several dBs, depending on the signal. This is why in Tables 7.1 and 7.2 the average PSNR produced is higher than the target PSNR.

For a target PSNR of 40 dB Fig. 7.5 and 7.6 show two delay signals before and after the compression. The error is also given for easy judgement of the reconstruction quality. For delay signals the achieved average PSNR is 42.15 dB. The average compression is more than 19 times.

Signal 10 (Fig. 7.5) differed from the rest of delay signals in the experiments because it is very bursty. The high burstiness of the signal makes it difficult to compress as it requires a lot of high frequency components to be preserved.

150

Target	Avg.	Min.	Max.	C.R.
44 db	46.82	44.06	50.73	11.39
42 db	44.68	42.06	48.00	13.06
40 db	42.15	40.06	46.16	16.09
38 db	40.45	38.08	44.06	18.76
36 db	38.23	36.50	41.44	22.74

Table 7.1: Target, Average, Min. and Max. PSNR values from 30 runs and C.R. values for delay signals.

Target	Avg.	Min.	Max.	C.R.
44 db	48.39	44.03	51.03	11.16
42 db	44.17	42.27	49.12	13.46
40 db	43.70	41.74	46.87	13.76
38 db	43.22	38.02	44.75	14.21
36 db	37.69	36.11	43.29	20.69

Table 7.2: Target, Average, Min. and Max. PSNR values from 30 runs and C.R. values for data rate signals.

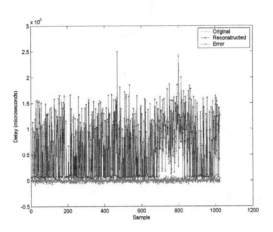

Figure 7.5: Delay signal 10 with PSNR=40 dB and C.R.=6.5

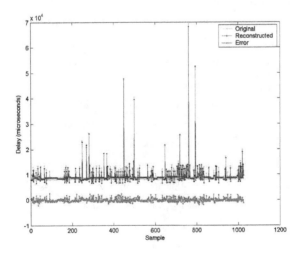

Figure 7.6: Delay signal 24 with PSNR=40.27 dB and C.R.=16.97

Similarly for the same target quality Fig. 7.7 and 7.8 show two data rate signals. For data rate signals the achieved average PSNR is 43.70 dB. The average compression is more than 13 times.

It is interesting to examine the results from the EZW algorithm against a non-transform technique. Bzip2 is considered to be an excellent tool for lossless data compression. Fig. 7.10 and 7.9 compare the sizes of the results from the EZW algorithm against the results of bzip2 applied on the original signals. On average for delay signals EZW achieves nearly 6 times more compression than bzip2 and for data rate signals 5.8 times. The target PSNR for EZW algorithm was 40 dB.

7.5   Comparison with GK based algorithm

In this section is presented a comparison of the results from the EZW compression method against the results of the GK algorithm presented in Section 5.3. There are only a few instances in both types of signals when the results are close enough to justify a comparison and they are presented in Tables 7.3 and 7.4.

Table 7.3 shows a comparison between the two different methods for similar PSNR values when examining delay signals. Similarly, Table 7.4 shows a comparison between the two methods for data rate signals when PSNR is similar and when C.R. is similar.

The EZW algorithm clearly behaves better when compressing delay signals as it gives higher C.R. for very close PSNR values. For data rate signals it is not as easy to derive a conclusion as in one instance EZW gives higher compression for similar PSNR value but for the optimum level of decomposition of the GK algorithm (level 5), GK gives much higher PSNR.

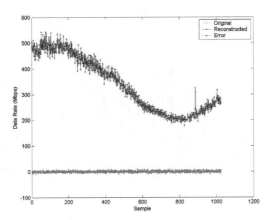

Figure 7.7: Data rate signal 20 with PSNR=44.5 dB and C.R.=13.67

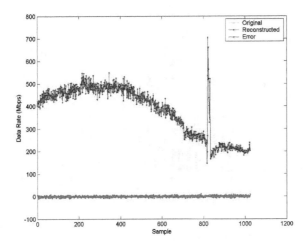

Figure 7.8: Data rate signal 16 with PSNR=46.86 dB and C.R.=12.97

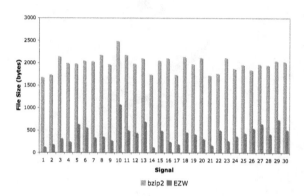

Figure 7.9: Compression performance of EZW against bzip2 for delay signals

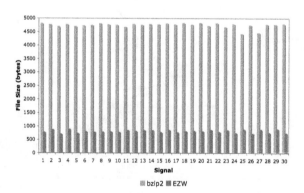

Figure 7.10: Compression performance of EZW against bzip2 for data rate signals

However, it is important to notice that the two compression mechanisms behave in a very different method when thresholding coefficients across the levels of decomposition. After the signal's decomposition the GK algorithm equally affects coefficients peculiar to each level of decomposition, i.e. the proportion of filtered coefficients is similar for each level.

On the other hand, EZW affects in a more significant degree lower levels where the coefficients do not attribute a significant amount of the signal's total quality. As the level increases, EZW's negative impact on the coefficients becomes less. As a result, the scaling behaviour in low levels is expected to display higher error in the reconstructed signal.

7.6 Summary

This chapter describes the embedded zero-tree algorithm, initially proposed by Shapiro, and uses it in order to perform lossy compression on computer network measurements. The algorithm first encodes the important signal characteristics and then encodes layers of detail until it reaches a user specified quality metric.

EZW can achieve high compression ratios by predicting insignificant wavelet coefficients across different scales while keeping detail in significant signal features and smoothing out the detail information in non-significant parts.

Due to the algorithm's feature of controlling the quality of the reconstructed signal, the results are consistent among different signals. The EZW algorithm comes as a solution to a problem with statistical based wavelet thresholding algorithms that discarded statistically "hidden" coefficients. Off-line experiments were run using real data rate and delay measurements.

Delay signals are compressed on average 16 times, that is 6 times more than bzip2 could achieve while achieving on average a PSNR of 42 dB. For data rate signals the average compression is 13.76 times, that is 5.8 times more than bzip2, and the average PSNR is 43.7 dB.

For data rate signals, EZW has a lower compression ratio as those signals include many more high frequency components and thus require more detail in order to preserve a high quality for the reconstructed signal. On the other hand, bzip2 results are produced by applying bzip2 on the ASCII files thus the results between delay and data rate signals are more consistent (Fig. 7.10). As for future work, the algorithm will be implemented in a real-time computer network-monitoring tool. A promising candidate seems to be CoMo.

In the next chapter, a possible additional benefit of the wavelet analysis is investigated. Specifically, an anomaly detection scheme for time series processes is described. Changes in time series processes reveal themselves in various frequency bands in the wavelet domain. By looking at the wavelet coefficients at various scales those changes can be detected.

EZW	algorithm	GK	algorithm
PSNR	C.R.	PSNR	C.R.
40.45	18.76	40.54	15.49
42.15	16.1	42	10.7
44.68	13.1	44.33	7.47

Table 7.3: Comparing results from EZW and GK for delay signals

EZW	algorithm	GK	algorithm
PSNR	C.R.	PSNR	C.R.
43.70	13.76	43.86	10.89
48.39	11.16	54.93	11.22

Table 7.4: Comparing results from EZW and GK for data rate signals

---

CHAPTER 8

Detecting Events in Computer Network Measurements

8.1 Introduction

Monitoring and measuring various metrics of high speed and high capacity networks produces a vast amount of information over a long period of time. These metrics describe the status and performance of the network in terms of utilisation, congestion, packets lost, etc. and help operators to identify potential problems.

For the collected monitoring data to be useful to administrators, these measurements need to be analysed and processed in order to detect interesting characteristics such as sudden changes. Identifying such characteristics in large amounts of data is a not an easy task and has been an interest of network researchers for many years.

Changes in networks cause changes in their performance and this is reflected in the collected measurements. These changes may occur due to change of load in the network, fault, or planned alterations in the infrastructure.

An automated tool for the data analysis and change detection phases would reduce costs required by the training and retaining of human resources. An example for the need of this tool comes from research conducted by the authors for the UKLight network. The proposed algorithm can be applied to network delay and data rate signals. Experimental results were obtained to examine how well the applied method detects changes in the signals.

A common methodology for detecting events in a network involves using historical data to estimate the mean and the variance and then flagging events outside the third standard deviation as anomalous [KRV04a] [KRV04b] [FSM93].

However, the time varying nature of a network should be taken into consideration. The performance of a network varies with respect to the time of day, day of the week, or season of the year. Thus, for a system to properly detect anomalies it should adapt to the dynamic nature of the network [FSM93].

In this work wavelets are used to adapt to the time varying environment of a network and detect any abrupt changes that are included in the measurements taken from that network. The advantages of wavelets as discussed in Section 3.5 make wavelets an appropriate tool for detecting sudden events in network computer measurements.

8.2 Methodology

8.2.1 Calculating the threshold

Because detail coefficients are actually changes of the average, those coefficients with large magnitude reveal a change in the original signal. In order to filter those coefficients that have a large enough magnitude to infer change in the original signal, a threshold is required.

For this task, a threshold based on the Donoho - Johnstone universal threshold (aka VisuShrink) [DJ94], [MMOP04] is utilised. For each level of decomposition the threshold is rescaled by a level-dependent estimation of the level's noise σ_{lev}.

Thus, the level dependent threshold is of the following form:

$$T_{lvl} = \sigma_{lvl} \times \sqrt{2\log_e n} \qquad (8.1)$$

Where n is the number of the total wavelet domain coefficients and σ_{lev} is the level-dependent noise standard deviation. As suggested by [DJ94], the median absolute deviation is used as a robust estimation for the noise standard deviation.

$$\hat{\sigma}_{lvl} = \frac{median(|cDetail_{lvl}|)}{0.6745} \qquad (8.2)$$

where $cDetail$ are the detail coefficients for level lvl.

8.2.2 Algorithm

For the analysis part, the Haar wavelet was used as the mother wavelet for the analysis because of the advantages listed in Section 6.4.

The methodology flow chart is presented below in Fig. 8.1. After applying wavelet analysis on the examined signal, the threshold (estimated as described above) was applied on *each level*. This step filters all coefficients that do not represent a significant change.

8.2.3 Estimating the position of a change

Some changes may appear at more than one scale but some others may appear only at one scale. This section describes the algorithm (Fig. 8.2) for estimating the position of a change depending on the number of scales that it is revealed.

In this phase, the notion of descendants, borrowed from Shapiro's Embedded Zero-Tree Wavelet algorithm [Sha93], is used. A coefficient at a coarse scale is named a parent and all coefficients at the next finer scale describing the same time location are its children. These children similarly may have other children coefficients that are referred to as descendants of the parent coefficient. Coefficients at the highest level are not descendants by definition.

The coefficients are scanned in a decreasing level order. First coefficients at the highest level are scanned. If a coefficient is found with a value not equal to zero, its value and position in the decomposition tree are stored.

Afterwards, its descendants are scanned. If a descendant is non-zero and has larger value than the parent, then its value and position replace the previous entries. Otherwise, the value and position variables remain the same. This process of checking the descendants is named "check descendants" as can be seen in Fig. 8.2 (the flow chart on the left of the brace). The whole process iterates in order to check all the descendants progressively down the decomposition tree.

When a descendant coefficient is scanned and has a non-zero value, it is recorded so it will not be scanned again as the scanning of coefficients continues in lower scales.

It should be noted that coefficients that belong in the lowest two scales of decomposition (Level 1 and Level 2) are not scanned during the above process in order to minimise false positive detections.

8.3   Off-line results

In this section, off-line experimental results are presented, i.e. the test signals were already captured from test beds and real networks as discussed in Section 4.6 and were later fed into the algorithm developed using the methodology and techniques discussed above. For implementation of the methodology, ®MATLAB and the Wavelet toolbox were used [MMOP04].

The proposed procedure detects the anomalies in the examined delay and data rate signals. In the following figures, the original examined signal is presented on top and the detected changes on the bottom of the figures. The significant coefficients produced after the thresholding, described in Section 8.2, are normalised and then plotted in the time instance that they represent.

Fig. 8.3 shows a data rate signal with four instances of significant change. All changes have been detected and plotted in the graph. The third change in the signal lasts for a longer period of time than the rest. However this is also reflected in the graph with high detection values in the time axis around samples 600 - 630.

In Fig. 8.4 a bursty data rate signal is presented that includes a big spike along some time samples (810 - 820). The anomaly is captured and plotted along the time samples that the change appears.

Fig. 8.5 shows another case of a bursty data rate signal with two spikes.

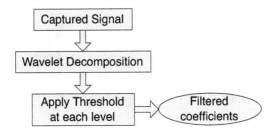

Figure 8.1: Algorithm Flow Chart

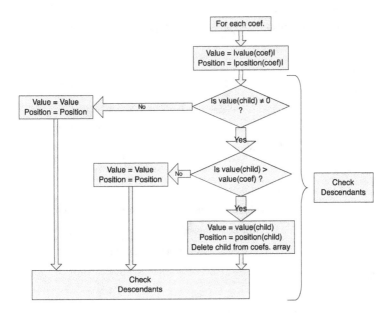

Figure 8.2: Algorithm for estimating position of a change

Both spikes are captured and accurately represented in the graph.

Fig. 8.6 shows a very bursty delay signal. The output of the detection algorithm has not identified any instance as significant. However, around samples 450 and 800 there are two instances that are set apart from the rest of the signal. Those two instances can be identified if the lowest two scales were examined. On the other hand, examining coefficients in these scales could increase false positives in the experiments.

Fig. 8.7 shows a delay signal with several spikes at the beginning and a region of burstiness later on. The algorithm detects the whole region of burstiness along with the most significant spikes.

In Fig. 8.8 another delay signal is pictured with eight spikes of different size. All of them are detected and accurately plotted both in time and size.

8.4   Summary

In this chapter a wavelet transform based signal analysis is used along with a threshold proposed by Donoho - Johnstone for detecting abrupt changes in computer network measurements such as delay and data rate. The signals examined were from real computer networks and not from simulation tools.

The time adaptive characteristic of wavelet analysis makes it a suitable tool for examining an environment that is time varying such as the computer network. Additionally, wavelet analysis can perform a local analysis and provide both frequency and time resolutions, which are necessary for the anomaly detection procedure. This would not be possible with the global representation offered from Fourier analysis.

After using the multi-resolution analysis capability of wavelets, the universal threshold is applied to filter those coefficients with a value large enough

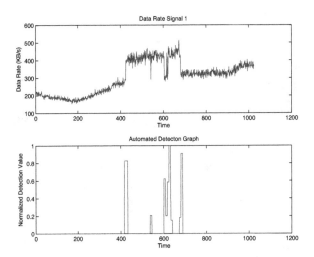

Figure 8.3: Detecting Changes in Data Rate Signal 1

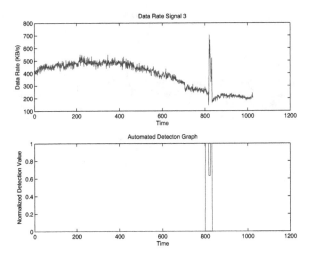

Figure 8.4: Detecting Changes in Data Rate Signal 2

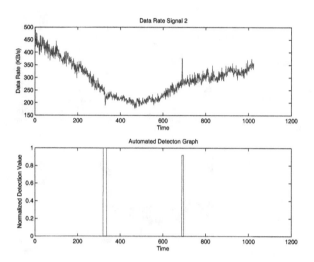

Figure 8.5: Detecting Changes in Data Rate Signal 3

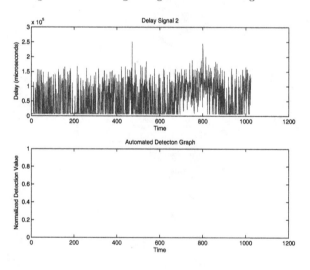

Figure 8.6: Detecting Changes in Delay Signal 1

167

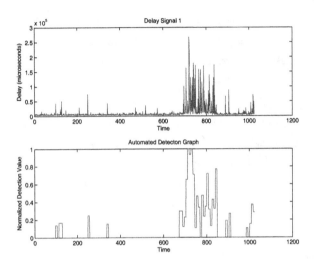

Figure 8.7: Detecting Changes in Delay Signal 2

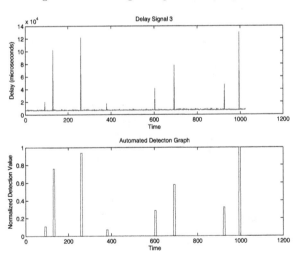

Figure 8.8: Detecting Changes in Delay Signal 3

168

to indicate a significant change in the original signal. In order to determine as accurately as possible the position of a change, the coefficients are scanned in a progressive way from the largest to the smallest scale. The duration of the anomaly is also indicated by the algorithm.

The calculation time of the algorithm is not an issue for the on-line implementation of the anomaly detection algorithm. This is because when analysing a data rate or delay signal where each sample is per second, a few milliseconds of processing time are adequate. Capturing such a signal of, say, 1024 measurement points would require 1024 seconds. Thus, there is a window of around 17 minutes for the analysis and detection phases to complete.

CHAPTER 9

Conclusions and Future Work

The performance monitoring and measurement of communication networks is an increasingly important area as demands on and threats to such networks increase. Monitored network data allows network managers and operators to gain valuable insight into the health and status of a network, and if interpreted correctly, can assist in planning upgrades and remedial action to keep the network operating in a near optimum manner.

Whilst such data is useful for real-time analysis, there is often a need to post-process historical network performance data. Such analysis is useful if ongoing long-term problems or if more detailed analysis of a previous situation needs investigation. Storage of the monitored data then becomes a serious issue as network monitoring activities generate significant quantities of data.

Compression of monitored performance data is an attractive option to reduce long-term storage requirements. However, selection of a suitable compression mechanism is a non-trivial activity. Conventionally, lossless compression algorithms have been utilised for this purpose, however it is generally accepted that higher compression ratios are achievable using lossy algorithms. These of course cannot support perfect regeneration of the original data. However, if the important and significant elements of the original data are preserved, lossy compression becomes attractive.

The work described in this book considers this issue and proposes the use of the Wavelet Transform as a first step in the compression of a time-series of delay or utilisation measurements. Using the Wavelet Transform in the manner described in the book allows useful further compression to be obtained over competing lossless algorithms, whilst providing controlled degradation of the signal. The degradation ensures that the important characteristics of the source data are retained.

Furthermore, apart from high compression ratios and good reconstruction signal quality, several factors of the compressed signal have been investigated in order to determine the effect of compression on them. The following list shows the goals of compression including statistical and quality aspects that should be preserved.

1. Offer high compression ratios

2. Quality characteristics

   - Preserve sudden changes: peaks and dips

   - High PSNR - Low Mean Square Error

3. Statistical Characteristics

   - Preserve Long Range Dependence

- Preserve Energy

- Preserve Mean and standard deviation

Two compression mechanisms were evaluated, named Kaur-Gupta and Birge-Massart, along with two threshold application techniques, soft and hard thresholding. In general, the BM technique increases the MSE and C.R. as the level of decomposition increases. On the other hand, the GK method restricts C.R. in higher levels of decomposition while keeping the quality of the reconstructed signals at reasonable levels.

The GK method is more appropriate for both types of signals as it offers more reasonable C.R. and good PSNR values even when reaching high levels of decomposition. It can adapt to bursty signals like in the case of signal 10 (Fig. 5.13) and it does not require any parameter like in the case of the BM method. The reconstructed signals preserve quality on interesting features while smoothing out the detail information in non-significant parts.

For the examined delay and data rate signals, hard thresholding technique performs better than the soft method regarding the reconstructed signal's quality. The compression ratio using soft thresholding is slightly larger, but choosing this method would increase the reconstruction error in much higher values.

The applied normalisation step in the compression scheme makes the storage of the wavelet coefficients more efficient, storing each of them with one byte without causing notable distortion while inverting the process to retrieve the reconstructed signal.

The GK algorithm has already been implemented by the author for CoMo. CoMo is a passive monitoring platform developed for the purpose of monitoring network links at high speeds and replying to real time queries. CoMo has various modules that each calculates one or more measurements. The

172

proposed algorithm is imbedded in the modules and compresses these measurements. When CoMo receives a query, the information is first decomposed and then shown to the end user.

Additionally, eight wavelets with increasing vanishing moments are compared for each of four different aspects: compression ratio, energy preservation, scaling behaviour preservation and quality of reconstruction. Due to the fact that each wavelet has its own characteristics and different wavelets approximate parts of the analysed signal with different degree of accuracy, the results vary with each wavelet.

The Haar wavelet, however, shows a consistency in describing better the analysed signals and has the best performance on average. In contrast with wavelets with many vanishing moments, Haar is conceptually simple, fast and memory efficient and it does not produce artefacts in the reconstructed signal. Wavelets with many vanishing moments increase the computation overhead, the complexity of the algorithm and the output file size.

An alternative method, proposed by Shapiro, in order to perform lossy compression on computer network measurements is the embedded zero-tree algorithm (EZW). The algorithm first encodes the important signal characteristics and then encodes layers of detail until it reaches a user specified quality metric.

EZW can achieve high compression ratios by predicting insignificant wavelet coefficients across different scales while keeping detail in significant signal features and smoothing out the detail information in non-significant parts.

Due to the algorithms feature of controlling the quality of the reconstructed signal, the results are consistent among different signals. The EZW algorithm comes as a solution to a problem where statistical based wavelet thresholding algorithms discard statistically "hidden" coefficients.

173

Finally, a threshold proposed by Donoho - Johnstone was examined for detecting abrupt changes in computer network measurements such as delay and data rate. The time adaptive characteristic of wavelet analysis makes it a suitable tool for examining an environment that is time varying such as the computer network. Additionally, wavelet analysis can perform a local analysis and provide both frequency and time resolutions, which are necessary for the anomaly detection procedure.

The proposed change detection algorithm can be implemented as a module in the CoMo platform as an on-line system. CoMo will be responsible for capturing data packets and producing measurements of the network, while the module of the proposed algorithm will detect anomalies in the analysed captured signal.

As was mentioned in Chapter 5 a characteristic of the Kaur Gupta algorithm is that it gives higher priority in preserving with higher quality sudden changes of signals (as in the case of signal 5.17). As a result, the algorithms rst priority becomes to preserve this characteristic and then comes the rest of the signal. In such cases the PSNR decreases and the C.R. increases relatively to signals which do not include sudden changes.

In order to have a better trade-off between C.R. and PSNR a hybrid approach could be applied where the time position of an anomaly is first detected and extracted and afterwards the compression is applied. After compressing the signal the extracted anomaly can later be reinserted in the time position of the signal from where it was extracted. With this method the compressing performance of the Kaur Gupta algorithm will offer more consistent results between signals that include and signals that do not include sudden changes.

For capturing and compressing packet characteristics, such as packet

174

length, the algorithm should be enhanced to perform faster due to the small inter-arrival rate of the packets in a 10 Gb/s network. This could be done by implementing in a dedicated hardware a faster algorithm of Wavelet analysis.

References

[ABF+02]   Patrice Abry, Richard Baraniuk, Patrick Flandrin, Rudolf Riedi, and Darryl Veitch. Multiscale nature of network traffic. *IEEE Signal Processing Magazine*, 19(3):28–46, May 2002. 3.5

[Agb96]   Johnson Ihyeh Agbinya. Discrete wavelet transform techniques in speech processing. In *Proceedings of the 1996 IEEE Region 10 TENCON - Digital Signal Processing Applications Conference*, volume 2, pages 514–519, Perth, Aust, Nov 26-29 1996. IEEE. 3.5, 6.2

[AKR]   Arun Avudainayagam, Prasanna Krishnamoorthy, and Krithi Rao. Jitter analysis in atm networks handling self-similar traffic. Website. Available on http://members.tripod.com/arun-10/selfsim/selfsim.htm. Page last visited 10/05/2007. 2.4.4, 6.5

[ARRE95]   Ralph Algazi and Jr. Robert R. Estes. Analysis based coding of image transform and subband coefficients. *Proceed-*

ings of the SPIE: In Applications of Digital Image Processing, 2564(XVII):11–21, 1995. 7.2.4

[AV98]   Patrice Abry and Darryl Veitch. Wavelet analysis of long-range-dependent traffic. *IEEE Transactions on Information Theory,* 44(1), January 1998. 2.4.4

[Ben05]   Tammam A. Benmusa. *The Processing and Interpretation of Communication Network Performance Data.* PhD thesis, Loughborough University, June 2005. 1.1, 1.3.1

[BKPR02]   P. Barford, J. Kline, D. Plonka, and A. Ron. A signal analysis of network traffic anomalies, 2002. 3.5

[CB97]   M. E. Crovella and A. Bestavros. Self-similarity in world wide web traffic evidence and possible causes. *IEEE/ACM Transactions on Networking,* 5(6):835–846, December 1997. 2.4.4, 6.5

[Cis06]   Cisco Systems, Inc. *Internetworking Technology Handbook,* 1992–2006. http://www.cisco.com/univercd/cc/td/doc /cisin-twk/ito_doc/snmp.pdf. Page visited on 7/08/2005. 1.2.1, 1.2.2, 1.2.2, 1.2.2, 1.2.2, 1.2.3

[CL]   Shihua Cai and Keyong Li. Matlab implementation of wavelet transforms. Website. http://taco.poly.edu/Wavelet Software/in-dex.html. Page last visited on 10/05/2007. 3.4.2, 3.4.2, 3.4.3, 3.4.3

[CM99]   Les Cottrell and Warren Matthews. Comparison of surveyor and pinger. Website, July 1999. http://www.slac.stanford.edu/ comp/net/wan-mon/surveyor-vs-pinger.html. Page last visited 10/05/2007. 2.1, 2.3.2

[Com99]   Douglas E. Comer. *Computer Networks and Internets*. Prentice Hall, second edition, 1999. 1.3.3, 1.4.5

[Con02]   FrontRunner Computer Performance Consulting. Computer performance metrics. Website, 2002. http://www. frontrunner-cpc.com/info/metrics.htm. Page visited on 7/08/2005. 1.4.7

[CYV00]   S. Grace Chang, Bin Yu, and Martin Vetterli. Adaptive wavelet thresholding for image denoising and compression. *IEEE Transactions on Image Processing*, 9(9):1532 – 1546, 2000. 4.1, 4.2, 4.2.1

[CZUM99]   Les Cottrell, Matt Zekauskas, Henk Uijterwaal, and Tony McGregor. Comparison of some internet active end-to-end performance measurement projects. Website, July 1999. http://www.slac.stanford.edu/comp/net/wan-mon/iepm-cf.html. Page last visited 10/05/2007. 2.1, 2.3.2, 2.3.3, 2.3.4, 2.3.7

[DJ94]   David L. Donoho and Iain M. Johnstone. Ideal spatial adaptation by wavelet shrinkage. *Biometrika*, 81(3):425–455, 1994. 4.2.1, 8.2.1, 8.2.1

[DJ95]   David L. Donoho and Iain M. Johnstone. Adapting to unknown smoothness via wavelet shrinkage. *Journal of the American Statistical Association*, 90(432):1200–1224, December 1995. 4.2.1

[DJKP95]   D. L. Donoho, I. M. Johnstone, G. Kerkyacharian, and D. Picard. Wavelet shrinkage: Asymptopia? *J. R. Statist. Soc. B.*, 57(2):301–337, 1995. 4.2.1

[Don95]   David L. Donoho. De-noising by soft-thresholding. *IEEE Trans-
            actions on Information Theory*, 41(3):613 – 627, 1995. 4.2.1,
            4.3

[DS98]   T. R. Downie and B. W. Silverman. The discrete multiple
            wavelet transform and thresholding methods. *IEEE Transac-
            tions on Signal Processing*, 46(9):2558–2562, 1998. 4.3, 5.5

[DS04]   M. S. De Silva. *Emergence in Active Networks*. PhD thesis,
            Loughborough University, 2004. 6.5.2

[DTRS01]   Arman Danesh, Ljiljana Trajkovic, Stuart H. Rubin, and
            Michael H. Smith. Mapping the internet. *Proceedings of Joint
            9th IFSA World Congress and 20th NAFIPS International Con-
            ference*, 2:687–692, 2001. 2.2.2

[ENW96]   Ashok Erramilli, Onuttom Narayan, and Walter Willinger. Ex-
            perimental queueing analysis with long-range dependent packet
            traffic. *IEEE/ACM Transactions on Networking*, 4(2):209–223,
            1996. 2.4.4

[Eur]   Réseaux IP Européens. Ripe – test traffic measurement project.
            Website. http://www.ripe.net/projects/ttm/index.html. Page
            last visited on 10/05/2007. 2.3.3

[fANR]   National Laboratory for Applied Network Research. Introduc-
            tion to the nlanr amp project. Website. http://amp.nlanr.net/
            AMP/. Page last visited on 10/05/2007. 2.3.5

[FGHW99]   Anja Feldmann, Anna C. Gilbert, Polly Huang, and Walter Will-
            inger. Dynamics of IP traffic: A study of the role of variability

and the impact of control. In *SIGCOMM*, pages 301–313, 1999. 2.4.4

[FGWK98] A. Feldmann, A. C. Gilbert, W. Willinger, and T. G. Kurtz. The changing nature of network traffic: Scaling phenomena. *ACM Computer Communication Review*, 28(5–29), 1998. 2.4.4, 6.5

[fIDACa] Cooperative Association for Internet Data Analysis (CAIDA). Caida: tools : measurement : cflowd. Website. Available on website http://www.caida.org/tools/measurement/cflowd/. Page last visited on 11/05/2007. 2.2.4

[fIDACb] Cooperative Association for Internet Data Analysis (CAIDA). Measurement infrastructure comparison. Website. Available on http://www.caida.org/analysis/performance/measinfra/evalta ble.xml. Page last visited on 1005/2007. 2.1

[fIDACc] Cooperative Association for Internet Data Analysis (CAIDA). The skitter project. Website. Available on http://www.caida. org/tools/measurement/skitter/index.xml. Page last visited on 10/05/2007. 2.3.6

[FSM93] Frank Feather, Daniel P. Siewiorek, and Roy A. Maxion. Fault detection in an ethernet network using anomaly signature matching. In *Proceedings of the Conference on Communications Architectures, Protocols and Applications*, pages 279–288, San Francisco, CA, USA, Sep 13-17 1993. ACM. 8.1

[GK02] Savita Gupta and Lakhwinder Kaur. Wavelet based image compression using daubechies filters. In *8th National conference on communications, I.I.T.*, 2002. 4.2.2

180

[HFW01]   Polly Huang, Anja Feldmann, and Walter Willinger. A non-intrusive, wavelet-based approach to detecting network performance problems. In *Proceedings of the ACM SIGCOMM Internet Measurement Workshop*, pages 213–227, November 1-2 2001. 2.4.4, 3.5, 6.5

[HV91]   Paul G. Howard and Jeffrey Scott Vitter. Analysis of arithmetic coding for data compression. In *Data Compression Conference*, pages 3–12, 1991. 7.2.5

[IDM+04]   Gianluca Iannaccone, Christopher Diot, Derek McAulley, Andrew Moore, Ian Pratt, and Luigi Rizzo. The como white paper. Technical report, INTEL, 2004. http://www.cambridge.intel-research.net/como/pubs/como.whitepaper.pdf. Page last visited 22/08/05. 2.4.5, 6.6.1

[Jar04]   Wayne O'Brian Jarrett. *Congestion Detection within Multi-Service TCP/IP Networks using Wavelets*. PhD thesis, University of London, 2004. 2.4.4

[Kapa]   Ian Kaplan. Estimating the hurst exponent. Website. Available on http://www.bearcave.com/misl/misl_tech/wavelets/hurst/index.html. Page last visited on 10/05/2007. 6.5.3

[Kapb]   Ian Kaplan. The wavelet lifting scheme. Website. Available on http://www.bearcave.com/misl/misl_tech/wavelets/haar.html. Page last visited on 1/2/2008. 6.4

[KFR02]   Thomas Karagiannis, Michalis Faloutsos, and Rudolf H. Riedi. Long-range dependence: Now you see it, now you don't ! In

Proceedings GLOBECOM '02, pages 2165–2169, November 2002. 6.5

[KGC02] Lakhwinder Kaur, Savita Gupta, and R. C. Chauhan. Image denoising using wavelet thresholding. In Subhasis Chaudhuri, Andrew Zisserman, Anil K. Jain, and Kantilal L. Majumder, editors, *ICVGIP*. Allied Publishers Private Limited, 2002. 4.2, 4.2.1, 4.3

[KKS+04] M. S. Kim, T. Kim, Y. Shin, S. S. Lam, and E. J. Powers. A wavelet-based approach to detect shared congestion. In *ACM SIGCOMM Computer Communication Review*, volume 34, pages 293–305, 30 August through 3 September 2004. 3.5

[KR03] James F. Kurose and Leith W. Ross. *Computer Networking: A Top-Down Approach Featuring the Internet*. Pearson/Addison Wesley, second edition, 2003. 1.1, 1.2, 1.3, 1.4.1, 1.4.1, 1.4.1, 1.4.1, 1.4.1, 1.4.2, 1.4.4, 1.4.6

[KRV04a] Seong Soo Kim, A. L. Narasimha Reddy, and Marina Vannucci. Detecting traffic anomalies through aggregate analysis of packet header data. In Nikolas Mitrou, Kimon P. Kontovasilis, George N. Rouskas, Ilias Iliadis, and Lazaros F. Merakos, editors, *NETWORKING*, volume 3042 of *Lecture Notes in Computer Science*, pages 1047–1059. Springer, 2004. 3.5, 8.1

[KRV04b] Seong Soo Kim, A. L. Narasimha Reddy, and Marina Vannucci. Detecting traffic anomalies using discrete wavelet transform. In Hyun-Kook Kahng, editor, *ICOIN*, volume 3090 of *Lecture Notes in Computer Science*, pages 951–961. Springer, 2004. 3.5, 8.1

[Li]   Yee-Ting Li. Grid monitoring schema. Website. Available on
            http://www.hep.ucl.ac.uk/~ytl/grid/monitoring_schema/ mon-
            itoringschema_03.html. Page visited on 7/08/2005. 1.4.5, 1.4.6

[LTWW94] Will E. Leland, Murad S. Taqqu, Walter Willinger, and
            Daniel V. Wilson. On the self-similar nature of ethernet traffic
            (extended version). *IEEE/ACM Transactions on Networking*,
            2:1–15, 1994. 2.4.4, 3.5, 6.5, 6.5.1, 6.5.1, 6.5.1, 6.5.3

[Mal98]   S. Mallat. *A wavelet tour of signal processing*. Academic Press,
            1998. 3.4.1

[MLA97]   Y. S. Mo, W. S. Lu, and A. Antoniou. Embedded coding for
            1-d signals using zerotrees of wavelet coefficients. In *In Pro-
            ceedings of IEEE Pacific Rim Conference on Communications,
            Computers and Signal Processing*, 1997. ISBN: 0-7803-3905-3.
            7.2, 7.2.3

[MM]   Matt Mathis and Jamshid Mahdavi. Diagnosing internet
            congestion with a transport layer performance tool. Web-
            site. http://www.psc.edu/~mathis/papers/inet96.treno.html.
            Page last visited on 10/05/2007. 2.2.6

[MMOP04] M. Misiti, Y. Misiti, G. Oppenheim, and J. Poggi. Matlab
            wavelet toolbox. Technical report, The MathWorks, Inc., 1997-
            2004. (document), 3.2, 3.3.1, 3.3.2, 3.3.2, 3.3.2, 3.4, 3.3.4, 3.6,
            3.3.4, 3.4.1, 3.4.2, 3.4.2, 3.4.3, 3.4.3, 3.4.4, 3.5, 4.2.1, 6.3.1, 6.4,
            8.2.1, 8.3

[Naw95]   David Nawrocki. R/S analysis and long term dependence in stock market indices. *Managerial Finance*, 21(7):78–91, 1995. 6.5, 6.5.1, 6.5.1, 6.5.1

[Nie99]   Yves Nievergelt. *Wavelets Made Easy*. Birkhauser, May 1999. 6.4

[NRIA03]   Abdul Mawla M.A. Najih, Abdul Rahman Ramli, Azizah Ibrahim, and Syed A, R. Comparing speech compression using wavelets with other speech compression schemes. In *Proceedings of Student Conference on Research and Development, SCORED*, pages 55–58, August 2003. 6.2

[Oet]   Tobi Oetiker. Multi router traffic grapher. Website. Available on http://oss.oetiker.ch/mrtg/. Page last visited 10/05/2007. 2.2.5

[PF95]   Vern Paxson and Sally Floyd. Wide area traffic: the failure of Poisson modeling. *IEEE/ACM Transactions on Networking*, 3(3):226–244, 1995. 6.5

[PMAM98]   V. Paxson, J. Mahdavi, A. Adams, and M. Mathis. An architecture for large-scale internet measurement. *IEEE Communications*, 36(8):48–54, August 1998. 2.3.1

[RNV06]   J. Ridoux, A. Nucci, and D. Veitch. Seeing the difference in ip traffic: Wireless versus wireline. In *Proceedings of IEEE INFO-COM 2006*, Barcelona, Spain, April 2006. 2.4.4

[Ros94]   Marshall T. Rose. *The Simple Book, An introduction to Internet management*. Prentice Hall, second edition, 1994. 1.2.1, 1.2.2

[Ros96]   O. Rose. Estimation of the hurst parameter of long-range de-
            pendent time series. Technical report, University of Würzburg,
            Institute of Computer Science, February 1996. Research Report
            Series 137. 2.4.4, 6.5, 6.5.1

[RRB01]   Vinay J. Ribeiro, Rudolf H. Riedi, and Richard Baraniuk.
            Wavelets and multifractals for network traffic modeling and in-
            ference. In *Proceedings of ICASSP*, 2001. 2.4.4

[RRB07]   C. Rolland, J. Ridoux, and B. Baynat. Litgen, a lightweight
            traffic generator: application to p2p and mail wireless traffic. In
            *Proceedings of the Passive and Active Measurement Conference
            (PAM 2007)*, volume 4427 of *LNCS*, pages 52–62, Louvain-La-
            Neuve, Belgium, April 2007. Springer. 2.4.4

[RW00]   R. H. Riedi and W. Willinger. Toward an improved understand-
            ing of network traffic dynamics. In *Self-similar Network Traffic
            and Performance Evaluation*. Wiley, 2000. 2.4.4, 6.5

[Sac]   Lionel Sacks. Case for support uklight monitoring and analysis
            at many scale. Website. 2.4.1, 2.4.2, 2.4.3

[San01]   Mark J. Sandford. *Detecting Changes in Network Performance
            from Low Level Measurements*. PhD thesis, Loughborough Uni-
            versity, July 2001. 1.1, 1.2, 1.4.2, 1.4.3, 1.4.5, 2.3.2, 2.3.5, 4.6

[SB04]   Joel Sommers and Paul Barford. Self-configuring network traffic
            generation. In *IMC '04: Proceedings of the 4th ACM SIGCOMM
            conference on Internet measurement*, pages 68–81, New York,
            NY, USA, 2004. ACM Press. 2.4.4

[Sew08]   Julian Seward. bzip2 and libbzip2. Website, 2008. Available on
            http://www.bzip.org/. 5.1

[Sha93]   Jerome M. Shapiro. Embedded image coding using zerotrees of
            wavelet coefficients. *IEEE Transactions on Signal Processing*,
            41(1):3445–3462, 1993. 5.7, 7.1, 7.2, 7.2.3, 8.2.3

[SL93]   J. Schönwälder and H. Langendörfer. How to keep track of
            your network configuration. *Proceedings of the Seventh Systems
            Administration Conference (LISA VII) (USENIX Association:
            Berkeley, CA)*, pages 189–193, 1993. 1.3.2

[SM96]   T. Saydam and T. Magedanz. From networks and network man-
            agement into service and service management. *Journal of Net-
            works and System Management*, 4(4):345–348, December 1996.
            1.2

[Smi06]   Steven W. Smith. *The Scientist and Engineer's Guide to Digital
            Signal Processing*. California Technical Publishing, 1997-2006.
            Available on http://www.dspguide.com/. Page last visited on
            10/05/2007. 3.1

[SP07]   Peter Sandford and David J. Parish. Traffic summary analysis
            for network abuse detection in high date-rate isp networks traffic
            summary analysis for network abuse detection in high date-rate
            isp networks. In *Proceedings of the Sixth International Confer-
            ence on Networking (ICN'07)*. IEEE, 2007. 4.6

[Sri03]   Deepika Sripathi. Efficient implementations of discrete wavelet
            transforms using fpgas. Master's thesis, Florida State Univer-
            sity College of Engineering, 2003. http://etd.lib.fsu.edu/ETD-

db/ETD-browse/browse?first_letter=S. Page last visited on 10/05/2007. 3.2, 3.3.1, 3.4.1, 3.4.2, 3.4.2, 3.4.3, 3.4.3

[ST99]   Z. Sahinoglu and S. Tekinay. On multimedia netowkrs: Self-similar traffic and network performance. *IEEE Communications Magazine*, 37(48–52), 1999. 2.4.4, 6.5

[Ste94]   W. Richard Stevens. *TCP/IP Illustrated, Volume 1: The protocols*. Addison / Wesley, 1994. 2.2.1, 2.2.2

[Sys]   Cisco Systems. Snmp v3. Website. http://www.ibr.cs.tu-bs.de/ietf/snmpv3/. Page visited on 7/08/2005. 1.2.1

[Tan03]   Andrew S. Tanenbaum. *Computer Networks*. Pearson, fourth edition, 2003. 1.3

[Tas01]   Robin Tasker. Requirements of network monitoring for the grid. Website, 2001. http://icfamon.dl.ac.uk/papers/WP7/netmon-requirements.htm. Page visited on 7/08/2005. 1.4.2, 1.4.3, 1.4.5, 1.4.6, 2.2.4, 2.3.2, 2.3.4

[TQD⁺]   Ajay Tirumala, Feng Qin, Jon Dugan, Jim Ferguson, and Kevin Gibbs. Iperf version 1.7.0. Website. http://dast.nlanr.net/Projects/Iperf/. Page last visited on 9/05/2007. 2.2.3

[VKMV00]   A. Veres, Z. Kenesi, S. Molnar, and G. Vattay. On the propagation of long-range dependency in the internet. In *SIGCOMM*, 2000. 2.4.4, 6.5

[VV06]   Kashi Venkatesh Vishwanath and Amin Vahdat. Realistic and responsive network traffic generation. *SIGCOMM Comput. Commun. Rev.*, 36(4):111–122, 2006. 2.4.4, 6.3.2

[WPRT01] W. Willinger, V. Paxson, R. Reidi, and M. Taqqu. Long-range dependence and data network traffic. In G. Oppenheim P. Doukhan and M. S. Taqqu, editors, *Long-range Dependence: Theory and Applications*. Birkhäuser, 2001. 2.4.4, 6.5

[YV04]   Byung-Jun Yoon and P. P. Vaidyanathan. Wavelet-based denoising by customized thresholding. In *International Conference on Acoustics, Speech and Signal Processing*, volume 2, pages 925–928, 2004. 4.3